THE GIFTS OF THE HOLY SPIRIT
IN THE DOMINICAN SAINTS

The Gifts of the Holy Spirit in the Dominican Saints

Ambroise Gardeil, O.P.

With an Introduction by
Romanus Cessario, O.P.

Translated from the French by
Anselm M. Townsend, O.P.

CLUNY MEDIA

THE THOMISTIC INSTITUTE

Cluny Media edition, 2016

This Cluny edition includes minor editorial revisions to the original text
including deletion of obsolete references.

Cluny Media has undertaken due investigation into copyright
interests in the materials included in this edition,
but copyright clearance is not a precise science.
Anyone claiming a copyright interest in this edition of
The Gifts of the Holy Spirit in the Dominican Saints
should contact Cluny Media by visiting www.clunymedia.com.

Nihil obstat:
F. D. McShane, O.P., S.T.Lr.
J. S. Considine, O.P., S.T.Lr.

Imprimi potest:
T. S. McDermott, O.P., S.T.Lr., LL.D.,
Prior Provincialis

Imprimatur:
† Samuel A. Stritch, D.D.,
Archiepiscopus Milwaukiensis

January 16, 1937

ISBN: 9781944418250

Cover design by Clarke & Clarke
Cover image: Filippino Lippi, *The Virgin and Child with Saints
Jerome and Dominic* (detail), oil and tempera on poplar, c. 1485
Photograph and permission by Fr. Lawrence Lew, O.P.

Contents

Introduction

Ambroise Gardeil, O.P., and the Thomist Commentatorial Tradition

A Treatment of Moral Theology

Not many readers of this small book will esteem that they hold in their hands a treatise on moral theology. I suspect, in fact, that most folks will be attracted to this title because they find themselves looking for authentic instruction in Catholic spiritual doctrine. True enough, we can learn a lot about Christian living, the spiritual life, or, more specifically, Catholic life, from Father Gardeil's classic treatment of the Gifts of the Holy Spirit. At the same time, the attentive reader will discover that the witness of the Dominican saints whom the author discusses supplies important elements of instruction about ethics and morality.

The moral dimension of Gardeil's work does not emerge as a curious happenstance, as if the author had chosen to include some edifying illustrations of the devout life by organizing his meditations on the Gifts around the lives of Dominican saints. Gardeil's purpose runs deeper than his providing grist for an inspirational mill. Why? Gardeil took his cue from a master of moral metaphysics. He learned about the true shape of moral theology from his teacher, Saint Thomas Aquinas. Truth to tell, Gardeil makes this point, though indirectly, when he assigns the architectonic Gift of Wisdom to the saint whom the Church acknowledges as her Common Doctor. The Gift of Wisdom shines forth in those persons who organize and conduct their lives according to the highest principle available to them. Wisdom, explains Aquinas, "denotes a certain rectitude of judgment in the contemplation and consultation of divine things" (*Summa Theologiae* II-II, q. 45, a. 5). Because of his affinity for divine things, the wise person achieves excellence in all things, including those matters that relate to the moral life.

All the saints are wise. They also point us toward heaven. By his appeal to the Dominican saints, Father Gardeil shows us how to live the moral life, that is, the everyday life of union with Jesus Christ that ensures the Christian's attainment of eternal happiness. The heedful reader will discover that Gardeil's presentation of the saints suggests less about his pointing out moral examples and more about our reaching the final end. What does heaven hold out for those who die in Christ's friendship? Heaven affords a contemplation of divine things that never ends. The Dominican saints who illustrate Gardeil's instruction about the Gifts transport us to that glorious reality where morality no longer operates. Heaven affords no option but to see God.

Heaven welcomes those who have done the will of God throughout the ages, those who have observed the commandments of God. While Gardeil's composition is not organized around the Ten Commandments—in fact, the word "commandment" does not appear in the text—this book provides sound instruction about how to keep the Decalogue. We learn, for instance, that one's living the Catholic moral life draws upon every capacity of the human person, intellect, will, and even the emotions or sense appetites. Indeed, Father Gardeil offers a complete instruction in moral theology. He teaches us more about being holy than about choosing rightly, more about the dimensions of Catholic life than about the rules that govern it. So he introduces us to a family of saints, a group of ordinary people connaturally made holy by God's grace.

Ambroise Gardeil (1859–1931) occupies a place in a Thomist heritage that enjoys more than seven hundred years of uninterrupted activity. In each period after his death in 1274 Aquinas's commentators have kept his teaching alive. They have passed along the important elements of his thought. The Thomist Commentatorial Tradition—the collective name for Aquinas's authentic interpreters—never lost sight of his placement of moral theology within the context of the virtues, the Gifts of the Holy Spirit, and the Beatitudes found in

Matthew 5. So it falls typically to Thomist thinkers to instruct people about the moral life by appeal to those saints whose lives embodied the Gifts of the Holy Spirit. The author of this work, an early twentieth–century Dominican, benefitted from the instruction that he had received from the French Dominicans who restored the Order after the ravages of the French Revolution. Indeed, Gardeil represents a moment of retrieval—one initiated by the papacy—of Aquinas's thought.

Throughout its long centuries of history, the Thomist Commentatorial Tradition has enjoyed moments of special ecclesial endorsement. Gardeil benefitted from one such moment. In 1879, when the young Gardeil was but twenty years old, the Pope, Leo XIII, issued an encyclical letter that called upon all Catholics to take inspiration from the work of Saint Thomas. This official document, *Aeterni Patris*, launched a remarkable renewal of interest in Aquinas and his commentators. Perhaps nowhere did theologians more vigorously take up the Pope's call than in France. Once Gardeil joined the Dominican Order, he became a leader of its intellectual life. So it happened that divine Providence inserted Ambroise Gardeil into a worldwide Catholic theological movement that held up for both inspiration and instruction the works of Saint Thomas Aquinas.

One did not have to wait for the political and social upheavals of 1789 to interrupt Thomist teaching. The Thomist vision of moral theology suffered a certain eclipse during the entire modern period, roughly from the middle of the sixteenth century to the middle of the twentieth century. Casuist moral theology, a mainly Catholic phenomenon that appeared after the Protestant Reform, offered a very different paradigm for Catholic life than what Aquinas had envisaged. Father Gardeil wrote during a period when moral casuistry dominated the life and practice of the average Catholic. Still, our author understood that, in this discussion of the saints and their Gifts, he was exposing important elements of moral theology that the standard moral theologians of his day ignored. Truth to tell, virtues, Gifts, and other refined spiritual endowments suffered displacement in the casuist handbooks. In fact, when *The Gifts of the Holy Spirit in the Dominican Saints* was first published, common cataloguing practice would have assigned the book to library shelves devoted to mystical, spiritual, or ascetical theology. Today, however, we realize that this gem of a book offers a comprehensive treatment of what Catholics should embrace and how they should live.

Mystic Mistakes

The nineteenth-century Thomist renewal and Gardeil's participation in it came none too soon. As students of Church history acknowledge, the late nineteenth and early twentieth centuries were not intellectually stable periods in *La Belle France* for the Catholic Church. Any number of good–willed but badly informed religious figures offered innovative proposals to make religion attractive to persons of modern sensibilities. Similar confusions arose elsewhere in Europe. Even in the United States, religion and mysticism came under suspicion as a result of the work of William James (d. 1910), who, one may note, deemed someone like Walt Whitman a healthy–minded religious person. It would be difficult to assert that Gardeil occupies a period that abounded in high instruction about the fine points of Catholic moral life and spiritual practices. In the early twentieth century, the rapid spread of devotion to Saint Thérèse of Lisieux and of her Little Way supplies the exception that proves the rule.

In France, a personage like Maurice Blondel (d. 1949) emerged as a philosopher bent on devising a new synthesis that purported to make Catholicism appetitive to modern consciousness. Observe that Gardeil published at Paris the French edition of the present book in 1903, ten years after the publication of Blondel's signature work, *L'Action: Essai d'une critique de la vie et d'une science de la pratique* (Paris: Alcan, 1893). Creative solutions that risked compromising Catholic orthodoxy were not limited to France. In England, Baron von Hügel (d. 1925) favored mysticism as a form of religious expression, but he also exhibited distinct sympathies for the suspect Catholic Modernists. In fact, the Baron sent his daughter for spiritual direction to the expelled Jesuit George Tyrrell, a priest who died under a cloud of condemnation. All in all, Modernism created uncertainties in the minds of both devout and less fervent Catholics. While Blondel, it is true, carefully put distance between himself and the Modernism controversy, his writings nonetheless moved away from classical Catholic teaching.

Ordinarily one thinks of Father Reginald Garrigou-Lagrange as the chief tactician for fending off whatever was misleading in Blondel's views. Ambroise Gardeil, his mentor and older Dominican brother, undoubtedly had sounded the alarm in the young Garrigou–Lagrange's head. The present volume witnesses to the perspicacity of Gardeil's spiritual insight. Because of his study of Aquinas, Ambroise Gardeil knew how to identify the false in popular ideologies. Today, in certain Catholic circles, one hears criticisms of the injunctions that the Church enacted against Modernist authors, including a rather recalcitrant figure such as Tyrrell. Sometimes observers cite Vatican politics to explain the forceful denunciations of Modernism that came over the signatures of Popes. However, the fact of the matter remains that Modernism developed among an elitist circle of putative savants whose insights favored the intellectual fashions of the period before World War I. Father Gardeil's instruction about the Gifts of the Holy Spirit is addressed to Everyman. The Dominican saints appear not as out-of-reach paragons of Christianity but as so many living proofs that divine charity infused into our hearts can make every believer eminently wise about the things of God.

Connatural Sanctity

Some of the saints that appear in this book may not be known to those who do not follow the liturgical practices of the Dominican Order. Catherine of Siena and Thomas Aquinas and perhaps Dominic Guzman himself will strike a bell in the minds of Catholics. However, the other saints probably remain foreign to many. It goes without saying that one does not need to know the details of each saint's life in order to profit from Father Gardeil's instruction. In fact the reader will discover the spiritual biographies of some great personages who have worn the black and white habit of Saint Dominic. The Dominican saints provide so many images of Saint Dominic himself. They reveal the virtualities of a man whom Divine Providence has chosen to sustain the life of the Church for more than eight centuries.

This edition of Gardeil appears in 2016, a year that marks the 800th anniversary of the papal approval that Saint Dominic received for his Order of Preachers. Dominican saints characteristically labor without toil. They demonstrate the connaturality of holiness, that is, they exhibit the way that the elevated life of grace attaches itself to our human nature and capacities. Grace perfects nature not by violent effort but by sweet embrace.

One feature of Thomist teaching that Popes have endorsed, stands at the heart of Thomist moral theology. Connaturality. Saint John Paul II, in his Encyclical Letter, *Veritatis splendor*, put it this way:

Indeed, in order to "prove what is the will of God, what is good and acceptable and perfect" (Rom 12:2), knowledge of God's law in general is certainly necessary, but it is not sufficient: what is essential is a sort of 'connaturality' between man and the true good. Such a connaturality is rooted in and develops through the virtuous attitudes of the individual himself: prudence and the other cardinal virtues, and even before these the theological virtues of faith, hope and charity. (§64)

Within a felt possession of divine grace, emerge the Gifts of the Holy Spirit that Father Gardeil so well explains in this classical Thomist instruction on the moral life.

~Romanus Cessario, O.P.
Saint John's Seminary,
Brighton, Massachusetts
August 12, 2016

Editor's Preface

"The Forgotten God" might well be used to describe the Holy Spirit. It would appear strange were it not that familiar things are least observed. The action of the Holy Spirit in our souls is so quiet and so continuous that it is barely perceived. The thought of the Father as Creator is overwhelmingly impressive. The sight of the Crucifix, the frequent attendance at Holy Mass, keeps the Redeeming Son ever in our minds. But the Holy Spirit, the Indwelling God of Sanctification, seems to be so intimately one with ourselves that we forget Him. Hidden He is, but that is no reason why He should be slighted.

Dominicans especially should have a deep vivid love of the Holy Spirit. He is the Spirit of Truth: we are of the Order of Truth. It was He who enlightened Thomas: we are Aquinas's disciples. There results a grave obligation upon us to have a devotion profoundly enlightened toward the Third Person of the Blessed Trinity. We must know who it is who acts upon us and how and why. Thus only can there be, as there should be, an intelligent co-operation on our part. So only can we "work out our salvation" with Him.

It is for this reason that we present as the third in this Dominican Library of Spiritual Works the present volume of Père Gardeil. Herein we may see the operations of the Holy Spirit in the up-building of Dominican sanctity. The saints are not isolated phenomena of the Order but the excelling types of that which should be of ordinary occurrence. They are ourselves as we should be, as we may be under the inspirations described by Père Gardeil.

The two opening studies require real thought since they deal with profound mysteries but they well repay the intellectual effort they demand. They are deeply theological, as must be any accurate statement of "the deep things of God," but they are written with a moving piety which refreshes during the processes of thought. The subsequent chapters, in which the author treats of the Gifts of the Holy Spirit in relation to the individual Saints, are marked by keen psychological insight, though, of course, other writers may very possibly differ from Père Gardeil in his attributions.

The saints, in fact all the just, enjoy all the Gifts of the Holy Spirit though usually one of them so predominates as almost to constitute a characteristic. Certain saints are, however, so multiple faceted that it is almost a matter of purely personal preference which prompts the selection of one out of two or more outstanding Gifts as the more controlling. In this connection, it would be interesting to speculate upon the characterization which Père Gardeil would have made of the universal genius of St. Albert, had he been canonized at the time this book was written. May this little volume contribute to an ever-deepening devotion to the Sanctifier, the Spirit of Truth, among the children of the Order of Truth.[†]

-Anselm M. Townsend, O.P.,
General Editor

[†] In the 1937 edition of *The Gifts of the Holy Spirit in the Dominican Saints*, published by The Bruce Publishing Company, this "Editor's Preface" appears as "Introduction."

Chapter I

The Role of the Gifts
of the Holy Spirit

The existence of the Gifts of the Holy Spirit in every just soul is a truth universally accepted in the Catholic Church. If no formal definition attributes to them an essence distinct from that of the infused virtues, nevertheless, excepting the theological virtues, they are presented to us as special supernatural perfections, superior to the infused virtues. They are given to us thus in the language of Holy Scripture and in the writings of many of the Fathers, the prayers of the liturgy, the growing agreement of Christian theologians and the voice of the Christian people.

What, then, is the place of the Gifts in the economy of our spiritual life? This is a question of supreme interest. Upon its solution depends the knowledge of what are, perhaps, the most marvelous of the operations of the Holy Spirit in our souls, the understanding of our supernatural duties, the most lofty as well as the most urgent. Equally dependent thereon, since God will not justify us without our consent, are the fruit and happy success of these divine operations.

Following St. Thomas and John of St. Thomas who, it would seem, has most profoundly penetrated his thought on this subject, we shall endeavor to give an account regarding the Gifts in the faithful soul. This study will be divided into two parts:

1.   What charity would be without the Gifts; and
2.   What charity is with these Gifts.

What Charity Would Be Without the Gifts

> "Verily thou art a hidden God, the God
> of Israel, the Savior."[1]

In this word *charity* we find our entire supernatural psychology concentrated. God dwells in us through sanctifying grace. He becomes the Guest of our soul. Our daily activity He controls by the infused moral virtues. The theological virtue of charity is, as it were, the point of penetration by which God, already dwelling in the essence of the soul, spreads over its power, and from this center He directs the operations of the infused virtues. It is through the heart, where there is gathered all that is unfolded in the activity of man, that God begins the deification of our intellect and will. The

---

1.   Isaiah 45:15.

infused virtues do no more than govern the good which charity has placed in the heart. Being the point of contact between grace and morals, or the seat of the whole supernatural psychology, charity vivifies the entire supernatural order.

At first glance, however, charity resembles all the infused virtues. Like them it is a supernatural habit. In the natural order, habit arises from repeated performances of an act and thus the natural virtues are acquired by the constant exercise of morally good acts. The supernatural virtues, on the contrary, are established in our faculties at a single stroke. God, infinitely powerful, dispenses with human activity which can do nothing in this regard, and inserts these divine graftings on the pristine native stock supplied by our nature. Sustained in being by the power from which it draws sap, the infused virtue transforms its activity. It enables our knowledge and our will to tend toward a divine good. Just as it is the property of a habit so to be at the disposal of the human will that its fortunate possessor may use it at will, so it is with the infused virtue. We freely make use of the Presence of God within us and of the communication of His own life which He has given us.

Charity, insofar as it is the proper effect of the Holy Spirit, surpasses all other virtues. Through grace the Blessed Trinity dwells in our soul. The Holy Spirit, who is love, finds a proper dwelling in the heart of man and it is charity that makes this abiding a reality. Herein lies the profound meaning of St. Paul's phrase, "The charity of God is poured forth in our hearts by the Holy Spirit who is given to us."[2] The Holy Spirit does not cause in us the love of God as an exterior agent which becomes foreign as soon as it has finished operating. He produces it as an interior cause dwelling in this love, for the Apostle says that "He has been given to us." His activity is like that of a soul, ever present in that which it does and whose operation never ceases. So long as the just soul loves God, it does not act alone; it has, deep in its heart, the Spirit of God, and it is this Spirit that causes the soul to utter, with all truth and efficacy, the name of filial love, "My Father!"

The soul of man is thus fully rectified by charity in relation to God, our last end. But it is in the order of things that the heart should radiate throughout its whole activity. In fact, the infused virtues, as faith and hope, prudence and justice, fortitude and temperance, operate under the influence of divine love. That is to say, that the Spirit of God, the soul of our charity, finds in these virtues channels by which He may spread the love which He inspires in the hearts of the just through all the parts of man, intellect or will, and even the passions themselves. Inspired by the Holy Spirit the prophet exclaims, "Bless the Lord, O my soul. All the powers of my soul, O bless His Holy name."[3]

Here arises a question whose answer will demonstrate the role of the Gifts of the Holy Spirit. In what

---

2. Romans 5:5.

3. Psalms 102:1.

way does the Holy Spirit, present in our hearts through charity, act upon our inmost psychology? In expanding, does it follow the laws of its own being or does it adapt itself to our Laws? Is its intervention in our action a simple uplifting of our psychological activity or is it an irradiation of what I may perhaps be permitted to call its own divine psychology? Is the Holy Spirit, present in our souls, the radiant sun whose rays pierce victoriously the thick clouds and whose power, directly and of itself, acts to enliven every creature? Or rather, does He, as with a cloud, envelop Himself like a beneficent prisoner in the forms proper to human action?

May we here apply to a subject so lofty the principles and laws which govern the natural order? Yes, for we follow St. Thomas who in many like cases has done so. In the sublime boldness of his strong soul in everything, he never thought that the supernatural order could be opposed to the natural. He never hesitated to apply to the former the conceptions of the latter, making them undergo only those modifications required by the perfection of their new state. First, then, we must answer that charity and the infused virtues are really and properly active virtues. Now, the active virtues essentially appertain to the perfection of the active human powers, and the Holy Spirit, dwelling within through charity, acts in us according to the manner of the human virtues, adapting Himself to the mode of action of our human faculties.

The just man, enriched with the supernatural vir-

tues, remains the true and principal author of his supernatural operations. He alone directs the movements of
his intellect and heart; his reason continues as the head
of his entire supernatural psychology. As a fire uncon-
sciously warming the heart, the Holy Spirit is strongly
but sweetly spread abroad in the faculties through the
virtues, or as a hidden light, illuminating without re-
vealing its source. It is "the fountain of life, the fire, the
charity and spiritual unction" (*Fons vivus, ignis, charitas et spiritalis unction*).[4] This changes nothing in the
ordinary functioning of our inner world, though everything is changed in regard to the end toward which
our activity tends and the vigor employed in aspiring
to it. Such is the role of the Holy Spirit inasfar as His
actions are performed by the virtues. He comes to us
as God—yet He is the "hidden God" of whom Holy
Scripture speaks.

From this arises the obscurity of our faith. In this
life we cannot have direct intuitive knowledge of es-
sences, and, if there is one especially which escapes our
grasp, it is certainly the Essence of God, the contemplation and love of whom is the very end of the supernatural order. Through revelation we are instructed
concerning the truths which pertain to this Essence
that, knowing it, we may desire it. But this revelation
is received blindly by our reason which is certified by
hearing, which is to say that it is through the testimony

---

4.   From the classic hymn, "Veni Creator Spiritus."

of God who neither deceives nor is deceived. From faith arises supernatural hope and love, which latter are nothing other than the habitual application of our hearts to the love of the divine good revealed through faith. Thus charity itself, entirely filled with the Holy Spirit who animates it and, as it were, weighed down by the omnipotence of the love which God has for Himself, allows itself to be ruled by the obscure knowledge of faith. The Holy Spirit is, so to speak, the prisoner of the imperfection of the love which He inspires. This constitutes the greatness of the respect which Providence has for our liberty, so strongly avowed is this plan of leaving to us, at least in the ordinary course of life, the merit of our justification.

If the theological virtues are regulated by man's narrow and limited mode of comprehension, with more reason this should be true in regard to the infused moral virtues. But the rational nature of man places the perfection of morals in a just mean, equally removed from the extremes of excess and default which may be found in the matter of his activity whether this activity be either exterior actions or interior passions. The loftiness of the supernatural end can raise the level of this just mode. It will not hinder it from consisting in the adaptation of human actions and passions to the supernatural end, which adaptation requires the reduction of the possible excesses of these human acts to the just proportion which makes them apt to reach their end. *To find* this just mean in relation to the divine end marked out by faith, desired by hope and willed by charity, is the role of infused Prudence. *To realize* the just mean already determined by infused Prudence in the domain of voluntary acts or the passions will be the roles of the infused virtues of Justice, Fortitude, and Temperance. Here again the Holy Spirit seems to sift through a sieve the brilliance of His action. Our entire practical moral order is governed by prudence as the order of conscience and the intentions was regulated by faith.

Thus it is apparent that obscurity and the just mean are the human veils under which the activity of the Holy Spirit is hidden. Without doubt this hidden action is infinitely precious to us, for by it we are ordained to the supernatural end. We ask: Will not the Holy Spirit, who has gone so far as to dwell within us, carry out His work to the end? Why, breaking through the uniformity in the regime of the virtues, should He not penetrate as Master into the soul of the just man, His servant? Why should not His intelligence and His heart, acting in their own way, neither contrary to faith nor prudence but surpassing them, sometimes become the immediate regulator of our acts?

We answer: Because it has not sufficed for the Spirit of God since the creation of the world, to be borne upon the waters, may the triumphant *fiats* shine forth again in the supernatural creation! May a new seven days arise and may the Gifts mark upon the foreheads of the just, like a radiant rainbow, the progress of the new divine work! *Veni, Creator Spiritus!*—Come, Creator Spirit!

What Charity Is with the Gifts

The Holy Spirit is the interior rule, immediate and homogeneous with our supernatural activity. Such is the ideal which is offered to the aspirations of the just. But no sooner has he grasped this ideal than his faith itself obliges him, not to revoke it, but to limit its extension. Should the divine intelligence become the proximate regulator of our inmost activity, this would be the unveiling in us of the Essence of God which is its object. But on earth we are not allowed to gain that insight which is reserved for the future life. God cannot on earth immediately regulate our moral world as an intellectual light without prejudice to that which He will become to us in heaven. It is only by a motivating influence that He intervenes in our life, and should the effect of this intervention sometimes be the expression of His intellectual life, yet it will be under the extrinsic form of an impulsive activity and consequently obscure. He will cause in us these effects of light under the guise of a secret instinct. No matter how enlightening divine revelations may be, faith, governed by charity, remains their directive light. (Prophecy must be excepted, but prophecy does not belong to the moral order of which we are treating.)

Is this direct influence of God upon our interior

activity possible? And, there being nothing opposed to it, does it exist? And if existing, under what conditions does it realize itself? These questions arise, and their solution will enlighten us concerning the role of the Gifts in our mystical life.

The positive character of the Aristotelian ethics as transferred by St. Thomas into the supernatural order appears at first glance to forbid every direct intervention from another world. What would become of the just mean in which morality consists should Prudence yield its place to the sovereign movements of external substances? Would it not lapse into an imaginary world, a revival of that of Plato, entirely under the immediate sway of Ideas and Exemplary Causes?

What then are we to think if Aristotle, ever opposed to Plato on this score, were to have taken the step? Would we not wonder if, in explaining certain men proposed as problems, this last disciple of Socrates, the tutor of Alexander, the rival of Plato, the admirer of Phidias did not confine himself to the ordinary and extrinsic principles of human character, but transcending reason went to the Divinity itself to seek the explanation of these divine men? In his *Nichomachean Ethics*, Aristotle writes of a manner of being which is superior to human nature, of a heroic virtue which, as it were, renders a man divine. This same thought he expresses in the Ethics of Eudemus in the chapter on Fortune. There are men who, without the aid of science or prudence, succeed in everything. How can we explain this? "It is asked," says Aristotle, "what is the principle of movement in the soul. It is clear that it is the principle of the movement of the world: a god…. The principle of reason is not reason but something higher. But what is there higher than reason which is not divine? It is not virtue, which is the tool of reason…it is not reason itself; the men of whom I speak did not use it; it is not enthusiasm, that has not this power. It is, then, without reason that they are what they are…it seems that the more the reason is absent the more scope the principle which directs them has for action: thus the blind have a better memory, disengaged as they are from that which distracts."

Thus for Aristotle, a heroic virtue, an extraordinary fortune or genius is due to the special and direct influence of the Divinity, the supreme reason of which the human reason is but a modest participation. In such wise he explains the deficiency of the rational commonplaceness of the morality of the just mean. His system makes reply to the difficulties which were raised by the Platonists in reference to certain personifications of humanity which go beyond the ordinary laws. Has he, perhaps, experienced within himself the impressions of the First Intelligence and does he so speak because he has felt its divine urges?

Yet, from the standpoint of contact with the Divinity, what are Socrates, Alexander, Plato, Phidias, Aristotle compared with the just man reformed by grace? If you are seeking sublime answers which illuminate as lights the dark depths of your tortured conscience, do

11

not ask Socrates but the child who has just made his First Communion. Does a glorious ideal fill you with enthusiasm, and do you live in a dream of conscience? If so, lay aside your Plutarch and ask that young man of clear and chaste look the secret of his heroic victories. Do not ask Plato concerning the life to come. He will underscore his sublime revelation with an enigmatic smile full of his own irony. Go, rather, and seek that poor woman who interrupts her work to enter that church; she will be able to tell you of heaven and what it has done for her. If you seek works of art, do not they surpass Phidias who form the resemblance in human clay of the very Face of God? If Aristotle seems great because he was twice raised to an understanding of the direct contact of the soul with the Divinity, yet what is that compared to the ordinary state of soul of a St. Augustine or a St. Thomas?

The Divinity inhabits the soul of the just through grace. It is well if it be a house prepared for the direct action of the Divinity. The just man is the natural sub-ject of heroic virtue. He is the one predestined to the touches of genius or marked as the object for divine favors. Hence, it is not astonishing that St. Thomas, inspired by the Philosopher, has judged it possible that God, the reason for the existence of our reason, should make Himself the immediate rule and inspirer of super-natural activity.

How can we know certainly whether the Holy Spirit substitutes Himself as the normal regulator of our supernatural life? We have only the one means to enlighten us, namely, the Word of God. The supernatural order is gratuitous in all its degrees, and the greatest arguments of fitness are not comparable in value to a single word spoken by God.

This word we have in Holy Scripture. We have already affirmed the faith of the Church in the existence of special, distinct gifts superior to the infused virtues. Holy Scripture gives us the characteristic trait of these Gifts. They are breaths, inspirations, *spiritus.* It is thus that it is said of the Messiah in the eleventh chapter of Isaiah "And the spirit (i.e., breath) of the Lord shall rest upon Him; the spirit of Wisdom and of Understanding, the spirit of Counsel and of Fortitude, the spirit of Knowledge and of Godliness, and He shall be filled with the spirit of the Fear of the Lord."[5] "Is not this language, which is habitual in Holy Scripture, clear," says St. Thomas, "and do we not therefore understand that these seven Gifts are in us by the divine inspiration?" There is no appreciable difference between that inspiration which is guaranteed to us by Holy Scripture and that instinctive urge toward good of those "foolish ones who are pushed on to good" of whom Aristotle speaks.[6] The authority of the Word of God thus coincides with the bold views of the Philosopher. Scripture says "divine inspiration" where Aristotle had said "divine instinct." As a counterpart the former describes the

---

5.   Verses 2 and 3.

6.   *Οἱ ἄν ὁρμήσωσι κατορθοῦν ἄλογοι ὄντες*

state of reason which corresponds to the divine instinct by the word "foolishness" *(stultitiam)* while Aristotle in the same place calls it "irrational" *(alogoi)*. Why is there such an agreement? Perhaps that same Divinity which inspired the prophet Isaiah also inspired the philosopher of Stagira. In any event, St. Thomas, seeing this agreement between the two texts, drew from it the doctrine which is the culminating point, the center of his supernatural ethics.

Under what conditions does this divine intervention operate? To us our supernatural moral activity appears to be dependent upon two prime regulators: reason perfected by faith, and the Holy Spirit. These two principles harmonize because the divine reason is the cause of our reason. Nevertheless, each acts in its own way, hence, in the presence of the divine operation, our reason suspends activity. It is replaced by a higher principle than itself.

Here a question arises. The Holy Spirit dwells in us through grace as reason does through nature. From the point of view of acting upon our psychological organism, however, it would seem that reason surpasses the Holy Spirit—presupposing we are content with the ideas thus far presented. Reason was created for the exercise of its activity having every portion of the psychological organism as permanent auxiliaries. These permit reason voluntarily and easily to regulate all its powers, and give it entrance into our interior world to underlie the moral virtues. The Holy Spirit, however, is all-pow-

erful and does not need pre-existing dispositions in order to operate. He creates the disposition by the very
fact that He acts. With Him everything is perfect; how
is it with us?

It is here, apparently, that St. Thomas goes definite-
ly beyond Aristotle. The latter had refused to recognize
a permanent basis for the special action of the Divinity
in the nature of man. For him, the entire foundation
of Fortune rested on the particular and unceasing at-
tentions of the Divinity. But St. Thomas found himself
confronted with a man already possessed of the Divinity, one in whom the Divinity habitually resides, whose
soul, as it were, the Divinity is. It is the property of the
soul to cause in the being which it vivifies all the organs
of which it has need. Why, then, should not charity
give rise to perfections and habits analogous to those
which make reason's entrance into the moral world so
easy? Can charity in the supernatural order refuse to
the just man what nature grants to man in the natural
order? Undoubtedly God does not need these points of
contact in order to activate my life. But for me it is necessary that He establish these contacts if I am to be as
perfect in the order of divine motions as in the rational
order. It is necessary that the inspirations of the Holy
Spirit be in me habitually just as the dictates of reason
are in me as a habit. I do not wish to give way violently
and as if constrained to God who encompasses my soul.
I wish to give Him place as the virtuous man yields
to his reason, voluntarily, readily, with that ease habit

15

alone can give. I wish to be able to say with the prophet: "The Lord God opened my ear and I did not resist; I have not gone back."[7]

St. Thomas makes a brief answer: the inspirations of the Holy Spirit are called "gifts" not only because God causes them, but because they constitute perfections which render man easily susceptible to divine inspiration. They are similar to those perfections which dispose him to receive the motion of reason in regard to his ordinary actions. This is equivalent to saying: If the direct intervention of the Holy Spirit in the government of our soul were merely spontaneous acts, as decrees, *motu proprio,* of the Holy Spirit, they would not have that permanent and definite character implied by the word "gift." Are not the gifts of God without repentance, like the gifts of man? It is necessary not only that the Spirit be "given" to us, that is, should be a habit in our souls, but that His inspirations should also be given and form for us one of the habits of our souls. How might this be? We should no longer be the active principle of these inspirations for they would remain only the inspirations of the Holy Spirit. On the contrary, we should be a passive principle, that is, the Gifts should place us habitually under their dependence. Thus, through them we should have a permanent right and hold upon the breathing of the spirit.

Truly this doctrine of the Angelic Doctor is admirable. For him, the doctrine of the Gifts is contained

---

7.   Isaiah 50:5.

in the two words, "spirit" and "gift." As the breathings of the Holy Spirit, the Gifts postulate the autonomy of their principle. As Gifts, the inspirations of the Holy Spirit have a habitual contact point in our souls. Actual grace, of course, is needed to stir up the will to make use of the Gifts. Actual graces, however, are the breath of the just and prayerful soul. May God give us the will to make use of the Gift, this new habit of the soul, and may the Holy Spirit descend when invoked! The Holy Spirit is ever ready to serve us. "We use the Holy Spirit," (*Utimur Spiritu Sancto*) say the theologians in an energetic phrase. In reality it is the Holy Spirit who makes use of us, with all the independence of His way of acting, but we, predisposed by grace, determine the moment when He shall take us as an instrument. We are like a child who receives the image of the sun in a mirror and can thereby control it at will. He does not possess the source whence it comes, yet it is at his service and he makes use of it to cause the beams of the radiant star to penetrate into places which escape its direct action and are lighted by the paler rays of diffused light. Such is the child of God adorned by the Gifts. Through these God shines freely across his whole moral and supernatural life, formerly lighted by the calm light of the virtues. How happy he is! "And night is my illumination in delights" (*Et nox illuminatio mea in deliciis meis*).[8] Being passive in relation to the Holy Spirit, he possesses Him

---

8. Psalm 139:11.

and uses the influence of this Guest as both slave and free. "Where the spirit of God is, there is liberty" (*Ubi Spiritus Dei, ibi libertas*).[9] "Whoever the Spirit moves, these are the sons of God" (*Qui Spiritu aguntur, hi sunt filii Dei*).[10] Such is the strange antinomy of which the Gifts appear to us to be the divine solution.

We now see what charity is with the Gifts. It is not that gentle warmth, that fervor of the virtues which secretly insinuates itself into our moral organism and which takes the human forms of our reason and love. It is the blazing center, making its envelope glow, radiant as the sun. It is the light of the Face of our God resplendent in the sevenfold ray which is His own. Truly it is beautiful! It is the very brilliance of Thy countenance, O Holy Spirit! This light rests upon us. "There is signed above us the light of your countenance, O Lord!" (*Signatum est super nos lumen vultus tui, Domine*).[11] Not yet lighting our forehead, nor fascinating our gaze as in the Beatific Vision, it envelops our heart. Like a sun whose rays come from it ceaselessly, our heart is actuated and renewed by the action of the Holy Spirit who enlightens our whole interior world, our truth, love, hope, justice, passions, all, that God may reign over all, directly and according to His own method. "That God may be all in all things" (*Ut sit Deus omnia in omnibus*).[12]

---

9. 2 Cor. 3:17.
10. Romans 8:14.
11. Psalm 4:7.
12. 1 Cor. 15:28.

Such is the role of the Gifts according to St. Thomas. Whence did the Angelic Doctor draw this teaching, as sublime as it is original? The symbolism of the Middle Ages regarding him was not in error. It loved to represent him with the positive, calm, and serene glance of the Peripatetic for whom the hour of vision had not yet come, but from his breast escaped a brilliance as if the divine charity which filled his heart could not conceal the divine fire which it imprisoned. It is the Holy Spirit, who, through the Gifts, has burst forth in this divine genius. *Deus! Ecce Deus!*—God! Behold God!

Chapter II

The Gifts of the Holy Spirit in the Supernatural Life

You, as pious, just, and holy souls, formed in the school of the Blessed Dominic, aspire to live the supernatural life. But what is it to live the supernatural life? In what does this life, which is yours, differ from your natural life? The difference lies in the end to which your every thought, action, and affection tends. The natural life has as its end your continuance in being, your relations of family, of friendship, of service. Not that all this cannot be elevated by grace to a higher end, but, of itself, it is all limited to earth and must perish with you. The supernatural life, on the contrary, is exclusively concerned with that which lives beyond the tomb with God whom we firmly hope some day to enjoy in eternal vision. In advance, it ordains all our vital activities to this definite and glorious end. And, since this end surpasses all the powers of our nature, since the power of God is absolutely necessary to cause us efficaciously to tend toward God, it is most just that we call such a life supernatural. It is beyond our nature because of the loftiness of the ideal which it proposes to us. It is beyond our nature because of the divine power which it requires, a power which we have not a single means of causing to descend upon us and which is a pure gift of God.

To understand this supernatural life, insofar as it is given us to possess it on earth, we must transport ourselves in thought into the Beatific Vision wherein this supernatural life attains its apogee and its integral realization. Here God is all in all—not the God of the Philosopher, the First Cause, the Perfect Being—but God as He is in Himself, God the Father, God the Son, God the Holy Spirit. The blessed behold the wonderful spectacle of the Father begetting the Son through all eternity. They witness the Son, the Word of the Father, springing forth from His bosom like the splendor springing from a glowing sun without leaving Him, remaining attached to Him, ceaselessly plunging into Him to shine again and forever. They see the Holy Spirit, the mutual love of the Father and the Son. This love is the fruit of the perfect knowledge the Source, who is the Father, has of the Splendor, who is the Son and which the Son, who is the image of the Father, has of the uncreated Source of His own Beauty. The blessed behold the inmost essence of the Divinity, see in their first origin all those perfections of the creature which enchant us—being, goodness, truth, duration, unity, harmony, knowledge, heart, will, justice, mercy. They see them no longer scattered and crumbling as we see them, compelling us to consider them a group only at a time, but united and concentrated in the simplicity of the divine being, not diminished and darkened by created life, but in their full unfolding, all new and sparkling with the infinite life in which they remain plunged. This is but a feeble notion of what the blessed see face to face without comprehending its immensity, since it is boundless. There is nothing which touches, draws, or enchants us upon this earth, nothing of the good and the beautiful, which is not found in the ocean of the Divinity though infinitely enlarged, infinitely more beautiful and more consoling.

In the presence of this spectacle, the eye and the heart are open wide and the Infinite penetrates them without difficulty. Just as we allow ourselves, without resistance, to be penetrated by the good things of this world, the scholar by truth, the artist by harmony, the friend by the thought of his friend, giving them a permanent home in the depths of our very selves, so that they dwell and remain intimately and profoundly there in a way as true as that offered by material dwelling together, just so does God penetrate into the inmost recesses of the blessed. There He dwells and remains. It is a spiritual habitation of which lively thought and love form the foundation, the roof, and the walls. It is the only dwelling in which can live the incorporeal Being, the Pure Spirit, the Subsistent Thought and Love who is God. Such is the supernatural life when achieved, the life eternal in heaven.

To grasp what the supernatural life is on earth, it will be enough slightly to modify what we have just described. The life eternal is in the order of things accomplished what the present supernatural life is in the order of things which have not yet reached their conclusion though tending efficaciously toward that goal. Let me explain. It is the same reality which lies at the root of heavenly life and the supernatural life on earth, but, above, we possess it unveiled, never to lose it, while, here below, we have it veiled and may unhappily lose it. But, once more, apart from the difference between faith and sight, the possession is just as real. God dwells in our hearts as really as in the hearts of the blessed, since, in truth, we love Him and this love which we now have will not change after our entry into heaven. "Charity never dies," says St. Paul. Thus, the just man, the saint on earth, performs now, in the sight of God, the same triumphant act through which it will possess God in heaven. God already dwells in his love. His heart is a veritable heaven, although invisible and hidden from all eyes. Such, in its profound reality, is the supernatural life on earth.

But, to go still deeper into the springs of this mysterious life, who has been able to deposit this heavenly love in the heart of the man, living in the world? Of ourselves we cannot produce even a particle of love for God as He is in Himself. First of all, we cannot naturally know God in such a way: He must be revealed to us. But how can we love naturally what we do not know naturally? Further, even after He has been revealed to us, how dare we love Him? I mean with the love of friendship, a love given and received, in a word, an efficacious love, not the false and discouraging love which one has for an inaccessible being, a love which is only a shadow of love. Yet it is with this given and efficacious love that the blessed love God. God has stooped down to them and what they could not do He has given them the power to do. He has made them participants of the love wherewith He loves Himself. The divine act has become, so far as it is possible, the act of the blessed. And, as the Father and the Son love one another through the Holy Spirit, so the blessed love God through the Holy Spirit. But, since the love of the blessed for God is already in us in a state of efficacious tendency, it follows that God stoops down to us to make us participants of the love whereby He loves Himself, to raise our small love to the loftiness of His Heart. Thus it follows that the Holy Spirit, the consubstantial love of the Father and the Son, should, in a certain way, be at the bottom of our love of God. For, once more, we really love God, and it is by the Holy Spirit alone that one can love God.

The Holy Spirit, then, dwells in us in an especial way, though the whole Blessed Trinity dwells there as the object to which our faith and our love efficaciously tend. The Holy Spirit adds an especial way to this already intimate way of living in a soul. He resides at the bottom of the supernaturalized heart as the principle of the movement by which it tends toward the Holy Trinity. He is, so to speak, the heart of our heart. And, as the heart makes itself known in a man by an inclination which induces it, by a bias which orients it and draws it powerfully toward the good, so the Holy Spirit, as an inherent bias to our charity, orients us, draws us and carries us along toward the Holy Trinity, the common center of the aspirations of the blessed in heaven and of the just on earth.

It is with the expansion of this force, hidden in the depths of our supernaturalized heart, that the Gifts of the Holy Spirit are connected. They are one of the two ways, and the most divine one, by which the activity of the Holy Spirit operates in the souls of the just.

Every superior force has two modes of employing its action. First, it may raise up in the being subject to itself fixed, permanent organs which divide among themselves, under its direction, the various fields of activity which are necessary to attain the end which it purposes. It is thus that the superior force which we call a germ raises up in the living body an entire assembly of organs which divide among themselves the different functions of life. In this case the initial force conserves only the power which unifies and vivifies the organism; it does not intervene, directly and at every moment, in the detail of its work; it leaves each organ to act according to the laws which it has traced out for it; it seems to adapt itself to each one's mode of action.

It is thus that the Holy Spirit, residing at the source of our entire activity by charity, creates for Himself the fixed organs of its operations in the infused virtues, in prudence, justice, fortitude, temperance and in all the lesser virtues which are like the secondary organs, the tissues and cells of these supernatural organs. He contents Himself with unifying them, leaving them to attain their functions according to their special modes of action, analogous to those of the human moral virtues which bear the same names. The direction of the Spirit is not lessened by the power which He leaves to these ministers of His power, which hold from Him the vivifying impulse which forms the basis of the life of the just, which performs, noiselessly and naturally, works of a kind which are nonetheless divine since the Holy Spirit ceases not to be at their deepest source.

But if the vital force of the germ, essentially immersed in the matter to which it gives life, is in some sort exhausted in its first activity, such is not the case with a vital force which is independent and necessarily transcendent such as God is in relation to His creatures. The divine activity goes beyond the activity of all the organs which He has been pleased to create in order to realize it. Just as the head of a state, the absolute master of his realm, is not bound to act through subordinates in order to work his pleasure in such and such a part of his government, although, ordinarily, he allows them to act of themselves, so is the Divine Spirit who is the absolute master of the government of souls in regard to a supernatural end, the possession of the Trinity. We should expect, on His part, direct interventions, whether it be to aid the infused virtues, the ordinary organs of His government, for example, in certain extraordinary cases such as grave temptations which the ordinary virtue cannot overcome, or, simply because, being able, He wishes so to do, or to promote, here and there in our lives, works of an excellence which surpasses the common measure.

It is for these operations that the Gifts of the Holy Spirit serve as a base of operation. Of course, God could have justified us without our consent. He could have entered at will into our supernatural organization, making use of us as mere instruments for His work. Sometimes He so acts, and it is with operations of this kind that we must link, for example, the conversion of St. Paul and so many other interior miracles. It is with such operations that we connect prophecy, the gift of miracles and all those graces which are given to man not for his own sanctification but for that of others. But since He is concerned here with our personal sanctification, God did not will that, even if He acted upon us directly, without passing through the normal organs, we should be not only without merit but without co-operation with His spontaneous inspirations. Hence this sanctifying germ has caused the Gifts of the Holy Spirit to spring up in our hearts. By them our supernatural organism is, as it were, doubled. The extraordinary, the divine and spontaneous, is in some manner acclimated.

This disposition is truly worthy of a divine author for whom the extraordinary is the same as the ordinary, one who is truly wise and, if we may dare to say so, truly prudent in mind, absolutely free, knowing that in governing, He possesses infinite resources.

The Gifts of the Holy Spirit are not actual interventions of the Holy Spirit in our life, but habitual dispositions placed in our soul which lead it easily to consent to His inspirations. They are, the word is perhaps strange but exact, "disposabilities" in regard to God which the just soul keeps in reserve, after satisfying the ordinary duty which is incarnate in the moral task of the infused virtues. This is unquestionably an original and unique creation, but is not the case of a moral being who finds himself in possession of an end which absolutely surpasses him, under the divine directive influence itself, and which he is powerless to secure by his own powers, equally unique? Is it not necessary that, on this head, alongside the ever active virtues, there should be dispositions receptive of all those divine influences which the human activity cannot carry in its channels? Is there not need of permanent "disposabilities" in regard to everything which God may desire to work in him?

It is true that the Gifts of the Holy Spirit are limited in number, for there are but seven. Still this number does not exhaust the infinite resources of the divine bounty. Every time that the perfect number seven is used in theology to designate the works of God, it expresses not so much a limit as a plenitude. There are seven sacraments, seven virtues, theological and moral. There are seven sacred orders. Examples could be multiplied. Every time that the plenitude of the divine treasures are spread before us the number seven appears. It is represented before the Ark of the Most High, of Jehovah, in the seven-branched candlestick. We say, then, that there are seven Gifts of the Holy Spirit, fear, fortitude, piety, counsel, knowledge, understanding, and wisdom. Do not painters represent the splendor which escapes from the sun by a finite number of rays and do they not place some in relief of which they form the center and binding of each luminous sheaf? There are seven Gifts of the Holy Spirit, but the means which God has of activating us in regard to our end are infinite.

Thus the Holy Spirit, that Great Performer, from the depth of charity wherein He dwells, sees Himself performing upon the soul which is subject to Him, as upon a keyboard with many stops, here the activities, the infused virtues, there the receptivities, the Gifts. Behold Him, the Divine Orpheus, who sets Himself to the task. "The spirit blows where He wills." Under His impulse, the keys of the regenerated soul vibrate and there results a divine harmony wherein the vigorous chords of the virtues mingle with the intoxicating vibrances of the Gifts. In proportion as the divine harmonies spread, the luminous decisions, just actions, virile resolutions, chaste sacrifices, holy apprehensions, courageous attacks and unspeakable patiences, pious affections, prudent counsels, the laments of knowledge, the ravishments of understanding and finally, in heaven, the enthusiasm of wisdom, these surge, mount, and build themselves up into a sublime monument. And, in the depth of the hearts of the saints, the Divine Orpheus ceaselessly plays while the celestial Jerusalem slowly and majestically approaches from her coronation.

> Blessed City, heavenly Salem,
> Vision dear of peace and love,
> Who, of living stones upbuilded,
> Art the joy of heaven above,
> And, with Angel cohorts circled,
> As a Bride to earth dost move!
> Many a blow and biting sculpture
> Polished well those stones elect,
> In their places now compacted
> By the Heavenly Architect,
> Who therewith hath willed forever
> That His palace should be decked.
>
> All that dedicated city,
> Dearly loved by God on High,
> In exultant jubilation
> Pours perpetual melody:
> God the One and God the Trinal
> Singing everlastingly.[1]

---

1.   Office of the Dedication of a Church. Trans. John Mason Neale.

Chapter III

The Gift of the Fear of God

St. Louis Bertrand
St. Vincent Ferrer
St. Rose of Lima

It is to the honor of Christianity that it transfigures the human passions.

Is there anything whose rehabilitation can be more difficult than Fear? Love and hate, hope and despair, desire and disgust, anger, audacity...all these passions have a certain grandeur. But Fear...who would dare to take up its defense? Above all, who will attempt to find a place for this infamous sentiment in a moral code which respects itself and which respects man?

There is an initiative forbidden to human philosophy, which is always afraid that it has not sufficiently elevated itself. These pure moralists must have a doctrine of entire disinterestedness. What! Admit that men are sometimes afraid? Make use of it to urge them to good?

How shameful! Let us hide this wretched thing and, in order not to disarrange the good order of our pure precepts, let us suppress even its name from morality.

It is the Holy Spirit who must rehabilitate fear. It is true that the "fear" adopted by the Spirit has nothing in common with worldly fear. It is not the fear of men but the fear of God. "The fear of the Lord is the beginning of wisdom," say the Scriptures. And the Holy Council of Trent, confirming the age-long tradition of the Christian centuries declares that even the fear of the divine chastisements is something good and holy.

St. Thomas is not content with introducing fear into natural morality, considering it as the matter of a virtue, the virtue of the patient. It was not enough for him that fear should be considered as a legitimate motive to penance. This bold interpreter of the divine audacity wished to give it a place in theology which should be truly its own. Being unable to make a virtue out of fear because of that something irrational and, as it were, inhuman which it retains in spite of everything, he classifies it as a Gift of the Holy Spirit, that is to say something superior to reason, a direct emanation from the regulating influence of God upon human action. It is, then, as a Gift of the Holy Spirit that fear plays its important part in the supernatural Christian morality.

And behold, as if to echo this doctrine, men arise who dare to say aloud that they are afraid, that they consider fear to be an instrument of moral progress, of sanctification: men who make fear the inspiring thought of their life, who have the religion of fear. These men, nevertheless, knew not how to tremble before men. The just man of the old poet, "the just and resolute man" (*Justum et tenacem propositi virum*)[1] is but a child alongside of these great independents. In fact, by their strange behavior, they have come to represent the most sublime types of human morality made divine by the revelation of God. They are the Saints, the purest, most powerful, and the sweetest.

There are three chosen from the family of the Holy Doctor, the Doctor of the Gift of Fear: St. Louis Bertrand, St. Vincent Ferrer and St. Rose of Lima.

***

Had the profoundly pious artist who thought out the moving matins of the feast of St. Louis Bertrand read the tenth article of the nineteenth question of the *Prima Secundae*. The hymn begins with an untranslatable resonance of the sighs, the disciplines with which the Saint occupied his nights.

> *Nocturna coeli lumina*
> *Suspiriorum conscia*
> *Quae Ludovicus aetheri*
> *Mittebat inter verbera.*[2]

---

1. Horace, *Odes*, III.3.1.
2. The nightly luminaries of the sky are conscious of the sighs which Louis heavenward sent amidst the blows of his discipline.

The antiphons, the responses, the lessons begin a strange harmony wherein are mingled the words: tribulation, discipline, hair shirt, fasting, penance, death. Here and there cries, more vibrant and more keen, pierce the psalmody: "Burn here, O Lord, cut here, here spare not, that thou may grant pardon for eternity." Did fear ever attain a more poignant expression? Nevertheless, parallel to this plaint of fear there runs the song of challenge and of intrepidity. "He feared not the savage hordes whose multitude surrounded him. The stones, the spears, the arrows caused in him no fear." On the lips of the Saint were the words of the Apostle: "If I still please men, I shall not be the servant of Christ." Then the two songs, one of the fear of God, the other of the scorn of the world, end by harmonizing into one, the song of charity. With it mortification is transfigured. "Grant me, O Lord, to die for Thee as Thou hast died for me." And matins ends with a cry of triumph wherein all the rudeness of the impetuous waves of penance dies away upon the enchanting shores of glory: "Thou hast broken my hair shirt, O Lord, Thou hast surrounded me with joy that it should be my glory to sing of Thee."

***

If St. Louis Bertrand symbolizes the Gift of Fear in the service of personal sanctification, St. Vincent Ferrer represents it acting, so to speak, as an apostle. To this preacher it was not enough that he himself should fear

God. He desired that the whole earth should tremble with him.

He was a terrifying Saint whose whole words were ordered with the object of creating dismay. His favorite meditation was the vengeful Face of Christ coming upon the clouds of heaven. His gospel was the gospel of the end of the world. His meditation had considered, in advance, all its chastisements. He had paled before its just judgments. He was fearful because of this awe-inspiring Being. Like the traveler who, nearing the coasts of Sicily by night, beholds the peaks of the mountains crimsoned by a somber fire which reflects the hidden flares of Etna, so the face of this man, raised by the Spirit to that elevation from which one may discover the hidden horizons of the justice of God, reflects beforehand the avenging fires of hell. So lofty was he in the pulpit where he preached, so terrible, so penetrating the accent of his voice that one hesitated to believe him a man. His voice was the trumpet which sounded to summon both the living and the dead. He was the Angel of the Last Judgment.

***

With St. Louis Bertrand, with St. Vincent Ferrer, the Gift of Fear is still not wholly revealed. The mortified fear of the former is as the root of the tree hollowing the ground by its obscure and fecund labor. The active fear of the latter is as the trunk with its rough bark, overflowing with sap. In St. Rose of Lima, fear is as the flower which spreads around its perfumes and resembles a hidden and supreme homage to the hidden beauty of the Creator.

But do not look to find in St. Rose of Lima anything which resembles softness or affectation. Our Saint was a sturdy one and her mortification hardly yields place to that of her brethren.

But, upon the robust stem of expiatory fear, she raised in all its splendor the delicate and trembling flower of filial fear which, according to St. Thomas, dreads nothing so much as "not sufficiently to submit itself to God." Like the rose in bloom which the invisible breezes wave in the sunlight at the top of its stem, so is St. Rose before her Lord in the garden of the saints. And just as the rose seems to sum up, in its brilliant colors and unparalleled perfume, the highest and warmest energies of the sun, so this mystical rose sees blooming within her the whole of the light and warmth which the Holy Spirit infuses into the heart of the saints. Herein is insatiable purity; the humility which unceasingly studies and restudies itself; here we find the ever fervent prayer and, in every order of virtue, the need of the end, be it finite or infinite, for here both are as one. There is the perpetual ascent toward a likeness to the Heavenly Father; the anxiety not to lose sight of a single one of the features of His image; a delightful restlessness to reproduce them; a delicate search after all the nuances of the supernatural ideal. In a word, here is fear, filial fear of God, fear without terror, for it is a fear basically confident since it feels that it is due to the love of God. The soul realizes that the cause of every perturbation is that enough has not been done for God and that, in spite of all its efforts, the soul still remains at an infinite distance from the divine beauty of the Face of the Father who reigns in heaven.

Chapter IV

The Gift of Fortitude

St. Catherine de Ricci
St. John of Gorcum
St. Peter Martyr

"Who shall find a valiant woman?" Vainly do I look for the answer to this question in the Book of Proverbs where it is to be found. I see, indeed, an ideal description of this type of virtue, but this description stopped, the text is cut short and the Sacred Book ends. Is it a piece of irony or one of those eternally insoluble questions which the ancients call problems and we, enigmas?

Not so, it is not an enigma, or, if it be an enigma, it is solved day after day by the Spirit of God. To the weakness of Eve, He opposes the strength of the Mother of Sorrows; in contrast with the lamentable story of the inconstancies of women who do not place their confidence in God, He displays the epic of the holy women who have found in the inspiration of the spirit of fortitude the indomitable courage of heroes.

Such, it seems to us, was St. Catherine de Ricci.

Fortitude has two principal acts, supporting and attacking. These characteristics are rarely isolated. Nevertheless, as a rule, one of the two predominates. If we must make a choice, we would say that the temperament of our Saint was rather one of attacking. The Spirit of God inspired her with the knowledge, ability, and courage to act indomitably in His service.

While she was still a child she *willed* to become a Dominican. Immediately everyone had to bestir themselves to obtain permission from her father who was a personage of considerable importance in Florence; the Dominican who passed through the city, her uncle, Father Ricci, the Superioress of the Convent of Prato, who was related to the leading families and of great influence in Florence, all helped. The latter obtained permission for Catherine to spend ten days in her monastery. Naturally enough, at the end of the ten days, the Saint refused to return with her brother who had come for her. Her father hastened to the monastery, but the child would not return even with him: it was necessary for the Prioress to add her authority to his. Finally she set out, but only after making her return the condition of her leaving. Her father did not trouble to keep his promise. Thereupon Providence intervened and she fell sick "unto death." Her father was in despair. One day when he was weeping at her bedside and holding her feeble hand she said to him, "Father, Our Lord wants me to be His spouse. He has told me so. Let me go and I shall get well again. You shall see it." The father assented and the child suddenly recovered. This time she attained her end, her father permitted her to go. She had *willed* to become a Dominican: she was one.

Having become a Dominican she *willed* to become a perfect religious "up to the neck." "The nuns were proud to have a little saint as their companion, only they wished this little saint of eleven years old to stay on their own level, to be wise, amiable, obedient, regular, following along in the common rut."[1] This was the will neither of the Holy Spirit nor of His servant. The divine intimacies ravished her at her tranquil duties. Extraordinary phenomena multiplied. The troubled community was full of suspicions concerning these eccentricities. They went so far as to order her to spit upon these visions, but the latter, instead of disappearing, expressed approval. The exchange of hearts with our Lord, the stigmata and other supernatural manifestations were the reward of her obedience and the unequivocal sign of divine inspiration. Since she was the slave of the Rule, and of a noble and frank familiarity with all the sisters, she ended by obtaining the confirmation of her way of life. Her perseverance, her courage, her supernatural energy, never conflicting among themselves, won a complete victory. She had *willed* to be a perfect Dominican and so she was.

---

1. Louis Boitel, *Sainte Catherine de Ricci du Tiers-Ordre régulier de Saint-Dominique* (Desclée, 1897), 7.

But this was not enough. Herself perfect, she *willed* that her sisters also should be so. Now her valor was known and it was brought into evidence. First elected sub-prioress she surpassed all expectations, so much so that on the first vacancy she was unanimously elected Prioress. Thereafter she displayed her whole energy. A woman of the head as well as the heart, she ruled in a spirit of incorruptible justice…. An austere exemplar and vigilant guardian of the Rule, she allowed no fault to go unpunished. She would not tolerate her religious occupying their souls with frivolities or worldly affections."[2] Nevertheless her firmness was tempered with mildness as befits a gift of the Holy Spirit. Nature is violent: true fortitude is self-possessed and knows how to moderate itself. "Her command was so maternal that it was a great pleasure to obey her." We may judge that under this lofty direction the convent of Prato should become the home of the ideal religious life. She had *willed* that her sisters should be perfect and so they were.

Even this did not satisfy her. She now *willed* that the sanctity of the convent of Prato should radiate beyond it, upon the Order and upon her well-beloved Florence of which she was the protecting angel. Like St. Catherine of Siena she had disciples. "Her own Order gave her the first, Provincials and Priors called her their mother: religious of great importance were happy to correspond with her and to follow her counsels. Her whole family was in her hand…in the Florentine aristocracy she

2.   Ibid., 17–18.

could number a crowd of disciples, lofty souls capable of the most exalted Christian and civic virtues.... Most of them led a life in the world which would not have been out of place in the cloister." "Other souls, more perfect still, sought her friendship. It will suffice to mention St. Mary Magdalen de Pazzi, St. Philip Neri, St. Charles Borromeo, St. Pius V, and Savonarola. To the latter she always remained loyal and the convent of Prato became the home of his memory. Through her most extensive correspondence, the numerous visits which she received, through the edification which all received from their relations with Prato, she placed the seal upon the work of her life. She had *willed* that Prato should become a center of the perfect life and it was.

Thus, despite the greatest obstacles, the strong unity of this life is spread before us. The Spirit of God had taught her to *will* strongly that which He Himself willed and she *willed* it without faltering. Dominican Prefect, Teacher, Center of an Apostolate, such is the progress of her attack. She is the type of this first aspect of the Gift of Fortitude.

***

From Italy, the land of heroic condottieri, we pass to Holland, the land of the patient brave, the people who overcame with levees the encroachments of the sea, the ancestors of those heroes who but a few years ago calmly awaited the enemy in the trenches and, knowing not how to fear, won incomparable victories by simply not retreating. It is the land of fortitude, not so much that fortitude which attacks but that which sustains without weakening. The Divine Spirit, dwelling in souls by charity, often tempers His action in accordance with our natural dispositions and, since Charity knows how to suffer, *Charitas patiens est,* upon the soil of Holland we find ourselves in the presence of a race of saints of strong and patient charity.

For twenty years John of Gorcum had been pastor at Hornaer. All Holland was being ravaged by the Gueux. The Catholic religion had been destroyed over a large part of the land. In the parish of Gorcum, two miles from Hornaer, the Calvinists had taken prisoners a large number of priests, had shut them up in the citadel and subjected them to degrading outrages. John of Gorcum stayed in the midst of his parishioners: he wore secular clothes that he might be able to continue his ministrations. He succeeded in entering the prison of Gorcum to bring the Holy Eucharist to his imprisoned brethren. He took charge of the devastated parish. His comings and goings finally betrayed him. Made prisoner in his turn, he was shut up with the future companions of his martyrdom.

We cannot imagine the tortures which their tyrants invented. Stripped of their religious habits and half naked, they were transported to Brielle, a wearisome journey of some twenty hours. At Dordrecht they were welcomed by the populace which covered them with filth and heaped all manner of insults upon them. They were exhibited upon their boat like wild beasts for a certain price. At Brielle they were compelled to surround the banquet table of their executioners who celebrated their sorrowful victory by an orgy. The following day they were ordered to crawl on their knees to the place of execution and thrice to circle the gibbet. Believing that their last hour had come they sang the *Salve Regina* but it was nothing but a mockery. Through the midst of a shrieking mob they were led, to the market place where another gallows had been erected. Here another parody took place and they ended the day in prison. On the seventh of July they were summoned before the governor's tribunal and charged to abjure the Real Presence of Jesus Christ in the Eucharist and also the Primacy of the Holy See. Three of them succumbed but the others stood firm. On the following day one of the apostates, a Franciscan novice, returned to take his place among the saintly group.

It is the ninth of July, 1572. We behold a ruined Augustinian convent in the midst of whose ruins is an old barn whose dismantled roof is supported by beams. The Confessors of the Faith are lined up facing those. They are naked. The guardian of the Franciscans, Nicholas Pich, is seized first, a rope is thrown about his neck and he is hung from the beam. While he hangs writhing, a last attempt is made to induce the others to apostatize. John spoke and, on behalf of all, proclaimed the Real Presence of our Lord in the Eucharist and the Primacy of the Pope. Nevertheless two of them weakened. The others closed their ranks and stayed at their post of battle. One by one they were hanged, the rope around their necks tied to the beams of the roof. John of Gorcum was one of the last but his courage never failed. He was executed in his turn. From the gibbet nineteen corpses hung. The crowd rushed upon them, mutilated them, cut them in pieces; they placed the bloody limbs on the points of pikes and in hideous procession marched in every direction through Brielle. Finally all the pieces were gathered together in the market place and sold at auction to the highest bidders.[3]

In this sinister drama everything is resistance, sacrifice undergone, indomitable patience. There is none of the enthusiasm of attack. Fortitude is concentrated upon a single act, not to give way. In proportion as aggression grew sharper, the spirit of resistance became more intense. What spirit inspired in our martyrs those energetic refusals, those sublime denials, that heroic passivity? Nothing other than the Spirit of Fortitude, more admirable perhaps in patient endurance, wherein there is not a single human joy, than in the enthusiasms of activity. How great is the glory of those privileged souls whom God has called to suffering!

***

---

3. These details are taken from Daniel Antonin Mortier's *Notice sur Saint Jean de Cologne et ses compagnons* (Desclée, 1899).

48

Upon the floor of the Chapter room in the Convent of Bologna lies Peter of Verona. An accusing voice is heard. He is proclaimed for a dishonorable crime. The Prior invites him to justify himself. Kneeling, he refuses, simply protesting his innocence. The evidence seems to be convincing, however, and Brother Peter, driven from Bologna is sent to Iesi in the Marches. He sets out in disgrace and thus remains, for a long time bearing this divine trial without murmuring. At last the time comes when the truth prevails; his innocence is recognized and proclaimed and he returns to his convent, his face aglow with the aurora of the strong man who knows how to suffer with patience.

Now comes the moment for attack. Brother Peter is an inquisitor, that is to say he was charged with seeking out and following up heresy. He worked amidst the greatest perils. It is a mistake to believe that all the dangers were on the side of the heretics. Besides, it was chiefly by his preaching that he strove to convert them. So great was his boldness, so striking his success, that he became the object of all manner of ambushes. "I shall die at the hands of the heretics," he would often say, but he continued his mission without fear. In 1252 a plot was made to assassinate him. Brother Peter was warned of it. He announced to his brethren at Como that his end was at hand and told them that his martyrdom would take place between Como and Milan. Then, after a last discourse of farewell, he set out for Milan whither duty called him. Upon the road the ambush was prepared. The Saint sang with his companions the stanzas of the *Victimae Paschali Laudes.* He walked ahead with only Brother Dominic. In a thick copse the assassins rushed upon him and split his head open with a bill-hook. He said "Into Thy hands, O Lord, I commend my spirit." Then, summoning up his last energies, he wrote with his own blood these words upon the ground: *Credo in Deum.*

***

"Blessed are they who hunger and thirst after justice, for they shall be filled." This it is that really lay at the base of the souls of our three Saints. St. Catherine hungered and thirsted after the justice due to God, that is to say, the sanctity which makes the truly just soul. St. John hungered and thirsted after the justice which consists in doing one's duty and being faithful even unto death. St. Peter Martyr, who knew how to adore the justice of the God who chastised him when innocent, also knew how, without failing, to second the designs of that same justice when it struck error to safeguard innocence. Intrepidity in attack and patience in the service of God, such were the characteristics of our three Saints. Now they are filled in heaven whence injustice is excluded. They see, in its source, the divine will condemning the injustices of earth and approving every just intention. Let us, who suffer for justice and hate iniquity, raise our eyes and take fresh courage. The present strife is only for a time. There is a tomorrow after the day of persecution and martyrdom. The kingdom of God, the kingdom of justice whither our Saints have preceded us is very close to us. "Blessed are they who hunger and thirst after justice, for they shall be filled."

Chapter V

The Gift of Piety

St. Agnes of Montepulciano
St. Pius V
St. Raymond of Pennafort

Filial piety toward God is one of the characteristic traits of Christianity. Without going into the question, more subtle than important, as to whether it constitutes its whole essence, we should recognize that, in our religion, the worship of the Divine Paternity is placed in relief in an incomparable manner. Paganism and philosophy have honored the Creator, the Judge, Providence. We adore the consubstantial Father of our Lord Jesus Christ, who is also, by adoption, our Father and we call Him, in all truth, "Our Father who art in Heaven."

If, as the Apostle says, no one can utter the name of Jesus except through the Holy Spirit, it is so, with still greater reason, in the case of the name of our Heavenly Father. The Holy Spirit is at the head of our entire supernatural activity and, indeed, He must be, for how should we be able to perform acts reserved to God, such, for example, as the efficacious love of God, if God was not, by His example and His movements, the profound principle of our life?

"Among these virtues," says St. Thomas, "there is one which leads us to a wholly filial love toward God. It is this of which the Apostle speaks in the eighth chapter of the Epistle to the Romans, 'You have received the spirit of adoption of sons whereby we cry: *Abba* (Father).' Piety has precisely this effect of making us render to our parents that homage which we owe to them. When, then, under the influence of the Holy Spirit, we render to God the duty and the worship which we owe to Him as our Father, it is under the influence of the Gift of Piety that we act."[1]

The Dominican Saints have all possessed this spirit of children of adoption, all have acted under the influence of the Gift of Piety. If, then, we detach from the diptychs of the Order the names of St. Agnes of Montepulciano, St. Pius V, and St. Raymond of Pennafort, it is with no exclusive intention but because these Saints appear to us to display certain original aspects of the spirit of filial piety.

St. Thomas, in fact, teaches that the operation of the Gift of Piety is not uniform. In a family, love goes first of all to the father, the unit and foundation of the domestic society: but, by a natural movement, it radi-

---

1. *Summa Theologiae* II-II, q. 121, a. 1.

ates upon all those who, near or far, are connected with the family. The love of the father, the love of the mother, the love of the family, such are the typical manifestations of filial love.

But if God is the Father of the Christian family, Mary is its Mother, and the Catholic Church its complete expansion. It seems to us that the names of St. Agnes, St. Pius, and St. Raymond, respectively, symbolize these three aspects of Christian filial piety.

***

We are never more really in our position as children than when we are altogether little. But the Blessed Agnes was from the beginning an altogether little child of the Father. She entered the convent at the age of nine! But that which inspired her to do so was, nevertheless, not violence, caprice, feeling, nor imagination. It was a profound and supernatural inclination which was to persist and always to grow in the same way, a really evident mark of the intervention of the Holy Spirit. Was it not this same Spirit who inspired the holy child-martyr Agnes, the thirteen-year-old namesake and patroness of our Saint? "She was barely old enough to receive the death stroke, says the grave St. Ambrose with emotion, and yet she already had the means with which to conquer death." Religious life or martyrdom, is it not all one to the Spirit who breathes where He will? Indeed from that moment her death to the world was absolute, her prayer continual and her piety toward the Father in heaven was wholly confident and tender.

One astonishing thing is that this child was as perfect in other respects as she was pious. The practical faculties, even those of government, were not wanting to her. Just as some children, educated at home in the school of their father, early manifest those serious qualities which seem more appropriate in a more mature age, so was this little servant of the Eternal King. At fourteen years of age, the nuns already regarded her as their little mother. She was made procuratrix of her monastery and her administration was marked by a wise understanding of everything. At fifteen she is abbess of a neighboring convent. To the end of her life she was to be a superioress. It seems that the Master and Governor of all things had willed to mark with the resemblance of His Paternity this pious child whose sole ambition was to live in filial dependence upon Him.

The absolute type of filial piety toward the Father is our Lord, Jesus Christ. Intimate union with Jesus Christ always resolves itself into a more profound sentiment of respect and love for God, since the union produces the resemblance. But who more than St. Agnes was in profound and almost familiar union with Jesus? It is difficult, without misstatement, to describe in human language the delicateness and the loftiness of these supernatural unions. Holy Church, which has the grace and the mission to do so, has not hesitated to turn the office consecrated to St. Agnes into a bridal song.

Magnae dies laetitiae
Venerunt Agni nuptiae
Et Agnes Agnum sequitur
Sponsoque Sponsa jungitur.[2]

May we, then, evoke the sentiments of filial piety of the Son of God. Let us recall that incomparable prayer to His Father which St. John has preserved for us[3] and, keeping all due proportions, let us not hesitate to make it the expression and the pious sentiments on the lips of the Spouse of Christ.

St. Thomas who sees each of the Gifts of the Holy Spirit expanded in one of the Evangelical Beatitudes, is uncertain whether to apply the Gift of Piety to that concerning those who hunger and thirst after justice or to that concerning the meek.[4] He concludes by making the choice dependent upon the characteristics of the individual saints. In the case of St. Agnes there can be no doubt. It is meekness that presides over the acts of her piety toward the Father, meekness in regard to the Sisters over whom she rules, the poor she serves, the travelers to whom she gives hospitality, and the sinners she converts. God made known the meekness of His servant by surrounding her death with significant phenomena. "A most sweet perfume was spread around

2. The days of great joy, the nuptials of the Lamb have come, and Agnes follows the Lamb; the Bride and the Bridegroom are wedded.

3. John 17.

4. *Summa Theologiae* II-II, q.121, a. 2.

her. Even down to the linen wet with the sweat of her agony, everything exhaled an odor of incense which filled the cell."[5]

The odor of incense, the sweetest perfume—piety, meekness—what could more aptly symbolize St. Agnes?

***

On the contrary, it is upon the hunger and thirst after justice that the Gift of Piety in St. Pius V is based. War and worship are the salient points of his activity. The warlike spirit in him was born of piety. For the war which he declares is a holy war, war against the infidel without who threatens to overrun everything, war against the infidel within who threatens to corrupt everything. The liturgical spirit in him was born of a profound piety. It is the great liturgy of the Church which he endeavors to reform: it is, above all, the pious prayer, par excellence, the Holy Rosary, that prayer whose multiplied "Aves" mingle the name of the Virgin Mary, the Mother of the great Christian family, with that of the Father who is in heaven.

The Office which the Church dedicates to him is full of this alliance between the justice which knows how to appeal to the arbitrament of war and the piety which lives by faith. The Capitulum of First Vespers is, in some sort, an outline of this. "God will surround

---

5. Louis Boitel, *Sainte Agnès de Montpolitien, religieuse de l'Ordre de Saint-Dominique* (Desclée, 1898).

thee with the Breastplate of Justice and place upon thy head the miter of an eternal honor; He will show thy splendor to everyone under heaven, for this is the name which God Himself shall give to thee; the peace of justice and the honor of piety."[6]

At Matins, the figures, at once warlike and religious, of the Old Testament pass in review. Moses on the mountain stretching his hands over the conquered Amalekites, makes a striking image of the saintly Pope praying with all the members of the Confraternity of the Holy Rosary on the day of the battle of Lepanto; St. Michael overcoming the Dragon, might be a symbol of the angelic Pontiff who took the name of Pius solely to war against the impious. We understand how the noises of battle mingle with these manly praises. The zeal of his faith is the zeal of a warrior; his confidence is as strong as armor; his charity fears not the multitude of his adversaries.

Lauds connects with the piety of the name which he had chosen his prudent and reconstructive government, his justice in the repression of vices, the constancy, continence, abstinence, temperance, and all the virtues by which he won for himself his splendid victories.

He is the Prince of his brethren, the support of his flock, the strength of his people, repeats the Capitulum of Sext, while that of None, replying to it like an echo, discloses the secret of his power, that from his whole heart he has praised his Savior and loved his God.

---

6. Baruch 5:2–4.

The prayer of the feast, summing up and entwining in its supplication the two aspects of this great saint, expresses itself thus.

> O Lord, who to destroy the enemies of Thy Church and restore Thy divine worship hast chosen the Blessed Pius as Sovereign Pontiff, grant that we may be defended by his protection and that, remaining loyal in Thy service, after we have overcome our enemies, we may enjoy perpetual peace. Amen.

***

The Gift of Piety could not express itself in the same way in the little saint of Montepulciano and in the warrior Pope of the Rosary. "Star differs from star in glory." In his turn, the aged centenarian who saw his religious childhood begin in his fiftieth year, the scholar who, for an instant, took up the government of his order only to lay it down again, could not be pious in the same way as a vigorous soldier of Christ or a little nun. What characterizes St. Raymond of Pennafort is the cult of the Christian Family considered no longer in its Divine Head nor its Mother, but in itself, its spirit, its history, and its glorious remembrances.

Who, on his travels, has not met one of those old savants who devote their whole being to the search, discovery, classification, and publication of documents which recall the life and the glories of their native land, their province, their city, their hamlet, or their religious or earthly family? Does not this studious cult of family documents belong, in its way, to piety?

"He searches with piety," says St. Augustine, "who venerates Holy Scripture and does not prune away that which he does not yet understand."[7]

It is in this sense that St. Raymond was pious. Inspired by God, commanded by Pope Gregory IX, in middle life, he attempted the collection of the "Decretals" that is to say, all the texts, all the acts, the memories, the memorable days in the life of that great family the Catholic Church. The five books of the "Decretals" together with the Decretals of Gratian which they complete are today still the basis of the legislation of the Church, reformed and newly codified in the present Code of Canon Law. It is by them, to a large extent, that the ecclesiastical order has life, the social harmony which we twentieth-century Catholics enjoy without having to trouble ourselves with the labor necessary to secure it. St. Raymond stands in the middle of time, preserving the past and insuring the future, inspired as he was with a profound spirit of piety toward that family of which God is the Father and Mary the Mother.

Quidquid est alta pietate mirum
Exhibit purus niveusque morum

---

7. *Sermon on the Mount*, IV.

Sparsa summorum monimenta Patrum
Colligit mira studiosus arte;
Quaequae sunt prisci sacra digna cedro,
Dogmata juris.[8]

St. Thomas, truly prodigal in regard to the Gift of Piety, discovers in it a third analogy with the Gospel Beatitudes. He has already connected it with the beatitude concerning the meek and that concerning those who hunger and thirst after justice. Now he recognizes in it that of the merciful.[9] It is under this third aspect that St. Raymond appears to us. Does it not seem as though he had spent the best part of his life in the dry study of law simply to merit his becoming, in the office of Grand Penitentiary, the supreme organ of the Divine Mercies in the Church? The sincere piety which inspired him rendered him no less solicitous for the salvation of the least of the children of the great Christian Family than for the interests of the general government. How can we fail once more to recognize in this characteristic an excellent Gift of the Spirit of God?

---

8. "Pure and snow-white in his life, he shows every wonderful sign of a profound piety.... Diligently and with marvelous skill, he collects all the scattered decrees of the Popes, all the dogmas of ancient law that merit holy immortalization." Hymn taken from the Dominican Breviary.

9. *Summa Theologiae* II-II, q. 121, a. 2.

Chapter VI

The Gift of Counsel

St. Antoninus

To the eyes of human prudence life is a battle. The interests of men are opposed. The good of one is often evil for another. The more clearly we see into human affairs the better do we see the obstacles in the path of our best schemes, the more or less evident are the maneuvers which conceal the counter projects inspired by the interest of another, often from a most praiseworthy motive.

The diplomat, the administrator, even the ordinary man who is merely wary and prudent in the conduct of his personal affairs, must, then, it seems, acquiesce in the ill fortune of others and resign himself to pessimism in regard to men and to human sufferings.

It is not so with the prudence inspired by God. The Holy Spirit assists in the unfathomable Counsel of the Holy Trinity where, from all eternity, the interests of humanity and the world were decided: yet His name is Love. He whom Isaiah called the Counselor par excellence, "Consiliarius," entered upon His public life by applying to Himself the words of that same Isaiah. "The Spirit of the Lord is upon Me: wherefore He hath anointed Me to preach the gospel to the poor, He hath sent Me to heal the contrite of heart, to preach deliverance to the captives."[1]

Accordingly, St. Thomas, following St. Augustine, has the audacity to attach the beatitude of the merciful to the Gift of Counsel, to give pity for the unfortunate as the distinctive mark of those prudent souls whose diplomacy is directly regulated by the Holy Spirit.[2]

St. Antoninus appears to us to be the very incarnation of this prudence according to the Holy Spirit. To this the Church bears witness by recognizing in him the words of Job which form the First Lesson of his office. "When I went out to the gate of the city, and in the street they prepared me a chair. The young men saw me and hid themselves and the old men rose up and stood. The princes ceased to speak and laid the finger on their mouth. The rulers held their peace and their tongue cleaved to their throat. The ear that heard me blessed me and the eye that saw me gave witness to me: because I had delivered the poor man that cried out; and the fatherless that had no helper. The blessing of him that was ready to perish came upon me and I comforted the

---

1. Luke 14:18–19.

2. *Summa Theologiae* II-II, q. 52, a. 4, sed contra.

heart of the widow. I was an eye to the blind and a foot to the lame. I was the father of the poor."[3]

Does not this scene, in the picturesque language of the East, express that alliance between the prudence which hears and the mercy which blesses so characteristic of the Gift of Counsel?

But let us now rapidly follow this double manifestation of one and the same Spirit in the life of our Saint.

Prudent, wary, diplomatic, he was never more so than on the day when, as a mere boy, he knocked upon the door of the Convent of Fiesole. With one of those clear glances which mature age no longer knows, the youth had judged the world and recognized the vanity of those seductions which surrounded him in the City of Flowers. He wished for God and God alone and like the merchant who, having found a precious pearl, sold all his goods that he might buy it,[4] our precocious diplomat is prepared to give all that he might become a religious. The Prior of the convent, thinking to put off this frail and slender youth whom he judged incapable of the observances of the Order, said to him, "When you have learned by heart the contents of this book, we will receive you." The volume in question was the "Decretals," the fundamental code of ecclesiastical law. Nothing could have been more forbidding to the young intelligence of the postulant but he immediately took the offer under consideration. A year later he returned

3.　Job 29:7ff.

4.　Matt. 13:45ff.

with the "Decretals" and asked to be interrogated: his memory could not be shaken and he was admitted.

His genius, as a Doctor, perhaps dates from this first intellectual effort. "He is above all a moralist," says his biographer.[5] "If, in his *'Summa'* he concerns himself with Dogma, it is that he might draw therefrom principles of morals. In four successive pictures, which form the four essential parts of his work, he shows, as in a preliminary outline, the human soul in its primitive nobility, its immortal destiny, its gifts and its powers. Next, upon these pencil strokes shimmering with light he throws the shadow of sin, its causes, its disorders, and its shames: this forms the second part. Following this path, he goes into all its ramifications and shows its deformity in all the circumstances in which man may find himself. With a sure hand he traces out for each the line of duty toward God, himself, and his neighbor and ends by displaying the path which, above all others, will bring the lost and fallen soul back to its primitive nobility, namely, the grace of God, the Gifts of the Holy Spirit, and piety toward the Blessed Virgin.

"Even in his *'Chronicles,'* one of the first attempts at a universal history, St. Antoninus is still a moralist. That which he follows in the history of a nation that which he perceives and declares, is the sovereign action, directive and beneficent, of Divine Providence."

This practical bent of his spirit destined him to administrative tasks. As Prior of St. Mark's he stamped

5.   Daniel Antonin Mortier, *Saint Antonin*, 2.

upon his government the character of a superior prudence. Endowed with a sense of realities, he always regarded the supernatural end as the supreme reality. One example out of a thousand will suffice. His first administrative act was the reconstruction of his convent. "Cosmo de Medici was the treasurer, St. Antoninus the architect. Accustomed to the splendors of his own palace, fond of display and rich, Cosmo wished to build for his friend a vast and comfortable monastery. The Prior was adamant. He drew the plan, decided the dimensions and superintended their execution in order to prevent any surprises on the part of his treasurer."[6] The result was the remarkably religious cloister of St. Mark wherein elegance and simplicity of line vie with a thorough understanding of the exigencies of the home of religious, advantages whose importance cannot be overemphasized. If, as has been justly said,[7] the cells are too narrow, it should not be forgotten that each of them, by order of the Saint, was enriched by one of Angelico's frescoes, like a radiant opening on to the infinite horizons of heaven.

We must hasten along. St. Antoninus has become Archbishop of Florence. What can be more worthy of praise than the moderation of his habitual government or the vigor of his use of power? The friend of the Medicis, he, as a good republican, knew how to defend against them the rights of the Constitution and of the

6.   Ibid., 8.
7.   Ibid.

people no less than those of the Church. While still in his cell in the convent of St. Mark, Cosmo would come to visit him by night to discuss with him the affairs of the republic. Now, official missions were entrusted to him. Of these he acquitted himself with dexterity. "His sanctity was no hindrance to his ability in these matters and his companions were able to write to the Seignoury that its ambassador had succeeded wonderfully and had won universal esteem and sympathy."[8] Thus posterity recognized him henceforth only under the title of Antoninus the Counselor, "Antoninus Consiliorum."

Postulant, professor, prior of St. Mark's, Archbishop of Florence, counselor of the Medici and ambassador of the Republic, St. Antoninus himself is always the same. His practical character developed and grew with an impeccable progress and unity. Is not this the activity of a soul counseled by the counsel of the Holy Spirit? "The motion of the advising mind is from the one giving counsel," says St. Thomas.[9] God moves each being according to its nature. He moves the body in space and the angel in time. Why should He not act according to the temperament of the prudent of this world who entrust themselves to His direction?[10] What is there astonishing in the fact that the activity of the saints, although it still borrows the forms of human prudence,

---

8. Ibid., 24.

9. *Summa Theologiae* II-II, q. 52, a. 2, ad 1: *Motio mentis consiliatae ab alio consiliante.*

10. Ibid.

should appear superior to the uncertain diplomacy of men by the whole superiority of the counsels of God?[11] Herein lies the secret of St. Antoninus: In his heart the Holy Spirit dwelt. It was He whom he consulted and he could reply to the prudent of this world as did another heroine, herself inspired in the same way though in a very different vocation. "You have been to your counsel and I also have been to mine."

But that which especially flows from the counsel of God is pity for the unfortunate. Whence does this come?

Give me a man of real prudence, not that miserly prudence which concerns itself only with the small side of things, and let this prudent man of real breadth go deep down into the depths of himself. He will not hesitate to admit that a multitude of things are beyond him. "The thoughts of men are timid and uncertain concerning our providence" (*Cogitationes hominum timidae et incertae providentiae nostrae*).[12] Who, at this point, has not been forced to doubt his own perspicacity? How much more true is not this of supernatural prudence, of that prudence which has as its aim the defeating, by a holy strategy, of the ruses, ambushes and that entire incessant diplomacy of evil which aims at holding men back upon the road to eternal beatitude?

Against an enemy so powerful, so persevering, and so shrewd, there is needed something hardly short of an extraordinary talent, even genius. To equal evils so

11. Ibid., ad 3.

12. Wisdom 9:14.

great, to assure us and those over whom we have charge
of the advantage of certain progress toward the supreme
end, man is not enough: God is an absolute necessity.[13]

But how can we place God before our eyes? That
same lofty prudence which has forced us to recognize
the necessity of addressing ourselves to the counsels
of God for our supernatural guidance shows us the
means. If you desire to be forgiven, says Jesus Christ,
forgive: if you wish to be aided by God, help your unfortunate brethren.

By this beautiful doctrine, made luminous by St.
Augustine, the transition is brought about from the Gift
of Counsel to the beatitude of the Merciful. Doubtless,
at the bottom, the obligation to be merciful remains a
duty of Charity. But from another point of view, that of
prudence, perfect because it is divine, it appears to be
dictated by a lofty anxiety, pure and thoroughly understanding, for the interests of those who are entrusted to
us. "And then especially the gift of Counsel corresponds
to the beatitude of Mercy, not as one eliciting, but as
one directing."[14] In God the heart and the head are not
inevitably opposed. To love the unfortunate is the inspiration of a heart animated by charity; it is also the
best policy. For the good fortune of the merciful, says
our Lord, is that they shall obtain mercy. "How just
does it seem to be," says St. Augustine, "that he who

---

13. Ibid., ad 1.

14. Ibid., a. 4: *Et ideo specialiter dono Consilii respondet beatitudo
Misericordiae, non sicut elicienti sed sicut dirigenti.*

seeks to be helped should himself aid those less powerful than himself."[15]

What a contrast there is between the heartless pessimism of policy and that prudence which, without losing its character, resolves itself into the widest and most heartfelt feeling! What a distance there is between the suave and indulgent benevolence of the diplomat and that active compassion inspired by the Counsel of the Most High. It is the entire distance from man to God. It is also the whole difference between the Medici and Antoninus.

Not far from the Seignoury with its portentous ramparts, where only the great of this world, the Senate and the Five Hundred, might enter, the palace of the archbishop, which he himself had stripped of every luxury, was open to every unfortunate being. A bishop clad in clothing more coarse than that of the poor received them. On his bed there was "a cover so scanty and wretched that a gentleman, touched with pity, gave him another, finer and warmer one."[16] He sold it for his poor. Bought back and again offered by the Saint, he sold it on three occasions. "Often more than one distinguished personage had to wait until the holy man had consoled some ordinary beggars."[17] Owing to this easy access a man whose excesses he had reproved tried one day to assassinate him in his cell. Fortunately the

---

15. *The Sermon on the Mount*, I.

16. Daniel Antonin Mortier, *Saint Antonin*, 16, 16.

17. Ibid., 9.

dagger swerved. He gave away all that he had, and his charity, going beyond his own century, inspired him to found an organization for the relief of the bashful poor.[18] "Merciful toward the wretched, and gentle toward the lowly."[19] Compassion and love, these are the two characteristics which sum up his relations with the unfortunate and such for him was the climax of an intelligence splendidly endowed with a practical spirit and diplomatic qualities.

He is for us a valuable example. We each have some small exterior government to administer; at the very least, it consists in our relations with those with whom we come into contact, in the care of certain interests, in the direction of certain persons. The practical spirit has necessarily a part in our life. If we wish to be thoroughly practical we must be supernatural. And hence, like St. Antoninus, we must obtain help from God by pardoning our brethren in a common miserable state and by aiding them as far as our resources will permit.[20]

If we do this, God will inspire us with His counsels, for He has made it a rule to aid those who help the unfortunate. Our life unfolds beneath mean preoccupations, the hardly Christian sentiments which our daily life engenders, the fatal clashing of personalities, the divergence of views even the most reflecting, sometimes the most supernatural. We soar. The angels, says

18. Ibid., 27.

19. Office of St. Antoninus.

20. *Summa Theologiae* II-II, q. 52, a. 4, ad 1.

St. Thomas, consult God ceaselessly. Their life is the simple gazing upon the divine will each time they issue forth to act and during their action itself.[21] It may be ours also. St. Antoninus teaches us by his example that we may also give to our lives this supernatural unity, prudence, and wisdom of outlook, upon condition that we do not separate the two aspects of the Gift of Counsel and that, accepting the direction of God for our own use, we fulfill the condition which it suggests to us. We must have a true supernatural compassion, an understanding of service to our companions along the road, who are subject to the same sorrows and labors as ourselves during this great journey which we all are making toward eternity.

21.   Ibid., a. 3.

Chapter VII

The Gift of Knowledge

St. Dominic
St. Hyacinth

The gift of the apostle is not the gift of the doctor. The doctor studies and teaches an impersonal science. His object is Truth for Truth's sake. He searches out, in their remotest origins, the reasons for the existence of things, and if on these heights he encounters God, it is because God is the Cause of causes, the ultimate Reason of grace and nature. The Holy Spirit, in becoming the immediate rule of the intelligence of the doctor, through the instrumentality of the Gifts, does not change that which is in the nature of things. By the Gift of Wisdom He increases the capacity of the reason, He illumines faith, He enables them to accomplish their sublime task with a sureness and loftiness directly participating in the Divine Intelligence. It is to this Gift that St. Thomas owes that divinely right and sagacious judgment which accompanies him from one end of his work to the other, causes it to make the First Truth, God, or the Trinity shine upon the whole mass and each detail of natural or supernatural truth.

The knowledge of the apostle, on the contrary, cannot abstract from the souls which it is designed to convert. It is not always the loftiest truths which are the best adapted for this end. Of what value to me are your metaphysics and your research into the finality of things if I do not understand you? What have you gained if the provocative and inopportune raising of a too crudely preached truth offends my weakness? The souls to whom the apostle addresses himself are immersed in practical life, in its intellectual and moral errors. They are not accustomed to judge things according to the higher reasons. They must take things as they are. If you wish to make them rise toward God you must first have an exact knowledge of the things which preoccupy them, of the evils and errors among which they struggle. This is simply that we must make an intelligent use of the divine truth when we are called to the ministry of the apostolate. We must understand it in its reactions upon creatures; we must adhere to those reasons which, ordinarily, carry conviction to the souls we address, even if they be not the most profound. "Note carefully," says St. Ambrose, "how Christ ascends with the apostles and how he descends to the crowds. How could the crowd see Christ if He did not descend? It does not follow on to the mountain tops, it does not climb up to the peaks."[1] But the Gift of the Holy Spirit which communicates to just souls this divine knowledge of human things, of motives and reasons drawn from the creatures, the necessary mode of approach for the apostle, is, according to St. Thomas, the Gift of Knowledge. It differs from the Gift of Wisdom in this that, instead of causing us to judge things from the point of view of God taken in all His inaccessible profundity, it presents them to us in the light of some point of view reflected in the creatures, sifted, so to speak, and adapted to the use of every soul of good will.

***

The Apostolic St. Dominic was destined to represent this Gift of the Apostles in an especial way. Whether we consider his vocation, the books whence he drew his knowledge or the instrument of his apostolate, his ministry and his whole life appear to us marked with the stamp of the Gift of Knowledge.

His vocation is foreshadowed in that distant episode of his student life when a famine was raging in Palencia. Dominic sold his books, his treasure, saying "How can one study upon dead skins while there are men dying of hunger?" When one day a more fearful scourge, the scourge of error which poisons men's souls, was revealed to a heart thus disposed from on high, the whole of the knowledge which he had acquired during

---

1. "The Descent of Jesus," in *Commentary on Luke*, VI.

twenty years of silent study adapted itself to save them. Behold him on that night in Toulouse when the divine call was revealed to him in that discussion with the host he sought to convert. The same spirit which had wrung from his compassionate heart that cry of pity for the starving now animated him "to give the knowledge of salvation to his people." All the while he was conversing, he sought earnestly for some arguments which could affect his host. He made himself aware of his moral and intellectual condition: he wished to discover the common idea, the truth admitted by both parties, a ray of God still preserved by the misled spirit, upon which he could draw to rekindle the light. At this moment, unquestionably he would sell, as "dead skins," all the knowledge he had acquired by the labor and meditations of twenty years to find the right word, the decisive phrase, which would deliver and satisfy this soul.

Nevertheless, knowledge cannot be assimilated without books. There is a method of understanding study which is not sterile and there are books which greatly lend themselves to the inspirations of the Gift of Knowledge. What then were the books of St. Dominic? His biographers tell us that there were three.

First of all there are the Epistles of St. Paul, the Apostle *par excellence.* But is not this precisely one of those books in which the Gift of Knowledge most radiantly shines? Where can we find a more profound knowledge and a more lively sentiment of the miseries of man without God and of the causes which prevent him from returning to God? If the Apostle sometimes "speaks wisdom to the perfect" how much more often does he not "lower his voice" through fear of frightening the little ones? How superb are his outbursts when, laden with the souls whose whole infirmities, in the compassion of his heart, he has taken upon himself, he, with them, raises himself to God, finding in the very poverty which the creature endures the very reason of their enfranchisement! How often must not St. Dominic have pondered the words, "I have regarded all things as dross that I might gain Christ!"[2] With what emphasis must he not have repeated the cry of his chosen master, "I am certain that neither life nor death... nor things present nor things to come nor might nor greatness nor any other creature can separate me from the love of God which is in Christ!"[3] What light this must have shed upon the life of those souls who heard words so profoundly penetrated with the sense of the vanity of the things which held them in the vices of the flesh or the errors of the spirit!

His second book was the Gospel according to St. Matthew, that is to say, the Gospel of the Humanity of our Lord, that in which our Savior has most descended within our reach. It preaches of His divine pities, His numberless cures, His immense mercies. "You shall bind the teaching of the law as a pennant in your hand and they shall wave unceasingly before your eyes." St.

---

2. Cf. Philippians 3:8.
3. Romans 8:38–39.

Thomas connects this precept of Deuteronomy with the Gift of Knowledge.[4] St. Dominic fulfilled this to the letter when journeying alone, his St. Matthew in his hand, his companions saw him make frequent gestures as if he wished to surmount some obstacle which would turn him away from his meditations "and they attributed to this familiar meditation upon the Sacred Texts the marvelous understanding which he had of them."

The third book of St. Dominic was a thing apart which did not resemble the other two. One day someone asked him where he had learned all that he knew. "My son," he replied, "I have no other book than that of divine charity." It is there, indeed, that we must go to discover the secret of a divinely sincere knowledge such as that with which his whole life was impressed. To acquire that imprint we must revive our knowledge at the breast of that powerful aspiration toward God and toward souls in God which the Holy Spirit, who is given to us with it, spreads abroad in us. We must impregnate our ideas and our speech with that need of the Divine Good which is placed at the bottom of the heart of every Christian. We must feel and live that need for ourselves and for those to whom we are to speak. Then the Holy Spirit Himself, hidden in that aspiration animated by His breath, speaks in the apostle. Such was the secret of the knowledge of our Blessed Father, St. Dominic.

The stamp of the Gift of Knowledge is again found in the great instrument of St. Dominic's apostolate, the

4. *Summa Theologiae* II-II, q. 16, a. 2.

Rosary. That which makes the Rosary so powerful a lever is its basis, chosen with a remarkable knowledge of the organization of our human nature. The Rosary comes to lay hold upon us where we are struggling amidst worldly, sometimes dangerous, joys; amidst sorrows, sometimes unreasonable, often crushing, and nearly always badly borne; amidst earthly hopes of every kind. Joy, sorrow, hope, these are indeed the three shores against which our agitated soul beats in turn. Dominic knew this and with an insight of remarkable precision saw all human life enclosed within these three sentiments. Then he gently lifted this poor life toward better joys, hopes, sorrows; he does not crush us with the splendors of Sinai or of Tabor. He draws us with the vision of joys holily understood, or sorrows divinely borne and of true hopes. Without denying the troubles of the soul, he eases them, transforms them, and elevates them little by little. The soft prayers of the "Our Father" and the "Hail Mary" rise like the music of love which, at each repetition, accentuates its insistence. How great a knowledge of divine things, of the human heart and the secret of adapting them was needed to compose the Rosary! Who could know how to proportion the divinest remedies to the most human of needs and unite them, the one with the other, by that most efficacious and consoling of ties, prayer? Who but the disciple inspired by Him who, being God and having created man, knew at once all that God could be to man and all the need which man has of God?

So, throughout the entire life of our Blessed Father, we find "that manner of understanding and experiencing the creatures which causes one to despise them in their seductions but to love them with moderation in ordaining them toward God,"[5] a striking characterization of the Gift of Knowledge. But a still more striking, we might venture to say definite, sign of this assimilation is given to us in another gift of our Saint, the gift of tears.

St. Thomas connects with the Gift of Knowledge the beatitude of tears: "Blessed are they that weep, for they shall be comforted." The reason which he assigns is remarkable. Knowledge differs from Wisdom in that, in order to judge things, it adheres to reasons accessible to men, whereas Wisdom climbs higher to the ultimate reason of things. But when one perceives these ultimate reasons which are, in reality, the will, the providence, the wisdom, and the goodness of God, there results in the soul, the effect of calm, serenity, and peace. That is why the beatitude of the peacemakers is attached to the Gift of Wisdom. But, when we take as our starting point the knowledge of things created, although this knowledge reveals a radiance which comes from God, their imperfections are so numerous, evil frequently prevailing over good, that inevitably it is with tears that we envisage the sorrowful plight in which we find ourselves and in which our fellow travelers struggle. The knowledge of human things is the mother of all sor-

5. John of St. Thomas, q. 70, disp. 18, aa. 4–5.

rows: the profounder the knowledge the more abundant are the tears to which it gives rise; for it is the knowledge of our miseries.[6] The Preacher wept over human life which he had seen through. The apostle, inspired by the gift of God, wept in his turn, feeling the miseries in whose midst the souls whom he wished to save found themselves.

St. Dominic wept often. "He had so great a love of souls," says one of the witnesses at the canonization process, "that it extended not only to all the faithful, but also to infidels and even to those who were amid the tortures of hell, and he shed many tears for them." "He often wept in the pulpit" and, in general, he was filled with that supernatural melancholy which a deep feeling of invisible things produces. "He offered the Holy Sacrifice of the Mass with a great abundance of tears…when the course of the ceremonies announced the coming of Him whom he had loved best of all since his youth everyone perceived the emotion of his whole being as tear followed tear down his loving countenance."[7]

We could multiply these traits. The countenance of St. Dominic owes its particularly moving character to his special gift of tears which is the outcome of the Gift of Knowledge. The Saint is a scholar who also weeps. We well know both the tears of repentance and the tears of love: here we have the tears of a man who, thanks to

6. *Summa Theologiae* II-II, q. 9, a. 4.

7. Henri-Dominique Lacordaire, *Life of Saint Dominic* (London: Burns and Oates, 1883).

an outstanding intellectual gift, has penetrated into the true knowledge of the world, of men and of God, has attained insight into its misery and its goodness and, passing through the world, has turned upon it a glance wherein emotion clashes with serenity and the sadness of earth with the consolations of heaven.

Thus is he represented in the marbles of his tomb, by the traditional likenesses and the pencil of Angelico. But it is for his children to be living copies of the untranslatable expression of the Blessed Patriarch.

***

Such especially was his favorite disciple St. Hyacinth, the great apostle of Poland. He had himself clothed him in the habit of his Order. In St. Hyacinth we encounter the same love of Sacred Science, the same devotion to the Blessed Mother, the same zeal for the salvation of souls, the same sorrowful yet consoled glance upon men, sorrowful from the compassion which he felt at the sight of their miseries, consoled by the knowledge of the divine mercies. Something of the Father, has passed into the soul of the son with the habit in which he was clothed. It would seem as if the Mother of the Savior, the Virgin so beloved by St. Dominic, wished to consecrate that sonship by receiving St. Hyacinth into heaven upon the very day on which the Church celebrates her own entry into heaven, her glorious Assumption.

***

But it is not only the canonized saints, it is also the simple faithful whom St. Dominic invites to reproduce the traits of his sanctity. Whatever may be the use which our life shall make of knowledge, even if our share be only the catechism and that knowledge of men and things which life brings with it, we must remember that such knowledge may be the instrument of the Holy Spirit. There is in us an intimate current, a profound tendency which, coming from God, brings us back to God. Let us take notice of this movement which is the soul of our life and let us ask of God, who dwells in us, to turn it into an ever-deepening knowledge of what we are and what God is. This was the prayer of St. Augustine. "Lord, let me know myself and let me know Thee. Let me know myself that I may hate myself; let me know Thee that I may love Thee."

This is true knowledge, complete knowledge, the science of the saints. It is not without a certain sadness regarding natural things. But the holy figure of our Blessed Father tells us that it also has its consolations. He is the living proof of the Savior's word: "Blessed are they that mourn, for they shall be comforted."

Chapter VIII

The Gift of Understanding

St. Catherine of Siena

Blessed Raymond of Capua relates that at the beginning of her visions our Lord appeared to St. Catherine while she was at prayer and said to her: "My daughter, do you know who you are and who I am? If you learn these two things you will be happy: you are that which is not and I am Who am."

This, we think, gives us the characteristic of the Gift which the Holy Spirit gave to our holy sister. It is the Gift of Understanding.

There are four intellectual Gifts: Knowledge, Wisdom, Counsel, and Understanding. The three former operate in us according to the method of operation of the human spirit, i.e., by reasoning; the Gift of Understanding is present as a simple intuition, as a spiritual insight which goes beyond appearances, which penetrates, beneath the mere letter or the symbols into the hidden meaning and causes the hidden thought to gush forth.[1]

"The soul," writes Bossuet, "laying reasoning aside, makes use of a gentle contemplation which keeps it peaceful, attentive and susceptible of the divine operations and impressions which the Holy Spirit communicates to it; it does little but receives much; its' work is gentle yet most fruitful." This work is a "simple look, glance, or loving attention in itself toward some divine object."[2]

This, doubtless, is why, in our Order, God has chosen one of the women Saints, and not one of the men, to personify in an especial, though not exclusive manner, the Gift of Understanding. With the men, among whom acuteness of reasoning is the dominant intellectual note, the Gifts are connected with reason, thus Knowledge to St. Dominic, Wisdom to St. Thomas, Counsel to St. Antoninus. To a woman, more intuitive, more spontaneous, more instinctive by nature, belongs the Gift which corresponds more to instinct and feeling, for, if propositions are deduced, "principles are felt."

Doubtless, nature, of itself, cannot intuitively know the Truth of God, the Principle of Principles, who defined Himself, "I am Who am." But God makes it His

---

1. *Summa Theologiae* II-II, q. 8, a. 1.

2. Jacques-Bénigne Bossuet, *Manière courte et facile pour faire l'oraison en soi.* See the Catholic Encyclopedia for information on Bishop Bossuet, who was a brilliant theologian of the 17th century.

glory to perfect nature that by comparison His gratuitous gifts become the more outstanding. Why should
He not then reveal Himself to a holy woman in a way
appropriate to the tendencies of her sex? That is to say as
a principle whose truth needs to be felt rather than reasoned out, as "a God sensible to the heart," as Pascal says.

"My daughter, you are that which is not; and I, I
am Who am." It is not a long speech: the word of Christ
carries its proof within itself: it is concise, luminous as a
principle; we might call it one of those sentences of the
Divine Master which fill the Gospel.

"O how great is this short phrase and how widely
does this simple doctrine extend!" cries Blessed Raymond of Capua. "What great wisdom there is in so few
words! Who will enable me to understand them? Who
will reveal to me their secrets and enable me to measure
the infinite?" And, as if to exemplify in his own person
the profound difference between the genius of the theologian and the Gift of the Saint, he indulges in long
commentaries upon this saying of our Lord. Still, he has
to stop without having completely exposed it and to acknowledge that whatever he could say is already known
by anyone who has penetrated the meaning of the two
phrases: "You are that which is not: I am Who am."

No, reasoning cannot measure the infinite. But who
then will give us to understand them? Let us learn from
Bossuet: "God is He who is: all that is and exists is and
exists by Him: He is that living Being in whom everything lives and breathes. It is only necessary to consent to

and adhere to the truth of the being of God: to consent to the truth, this act alone is sufficient. Note that I say consent to the truth, for God is the sole true Being. To adhere to the truth, to consent to the truth, is to adhere to God, is to place God in possession of the right which He has over us. This sole act comprehends all acts: it is the greatest, the loftiest which we can perform."[3]

Only intuition penetrates principles. When the Divine reveals Himself to us under this abridged form it is fitting that reasoning should be laid aside. It must, as Bossuet again says, "resolve itself entirely into a simple glance." This simple gaze is the work of the Gift of Understanding.

But, it may be asked, amid the lights of intuition, what becomes of the obscurity of faith? St. Thomas himself asked this question. He answers that there are two kinds of objects proposed to our faith. First of all, there is the Divine Being and His mysteries. Then, there is that large number of truths ordained to the manifestation of the former: Holy Scripture is full of this kind of truth which forms the secondary object of our faith.[4]

The Gift of Understanding is able to give us a *perfect* knowledge of these latter. In the history of St. Catherine, numerous traits bear testimony of this, notably

---

3. Another excerpt from a sermon by Bishop Bossuet, which he gave to the Sisters of the Visitation, on the occasion of the death of their confessor. (Original title in the complete works of Bossuet: *Discours aux Filles de la Visitation le jour du decès de M. Mutelle, leur confesseur.*)

4. *Summa Theologiae* II-II, q. 8, a. 2.

that marvelous penetration of Holy Scripture which all her writings display. That marvelous verse, "*Deus in adjutorium meum intende*" becomes the subject of repeated meditations. The Psalm "*Jubilate Deo omnis terra*" throws her into inexpressible raptures. Even if I wished to do so I could not make an end of exploring this intellectual side of St. Catherine. Let us only cite one fact. Several days before her death, she said that "with the light of a lively faith she had seen and perfectly understood, in her spirit, that all that happened to her and to others came from God and had as its cause the great love which He had for His creatures." The "light of a lively faith," it is thus (and we shall give additional proof in a moment) that St. Catherine always called the Gift which produced the intuitions of her contemplations. Her own words bear testimony that this light was allied to the obscurities of faith.

In regard to the Being of God and the divine mysteries, faith is complete. Nevertheless, according to St. Thomas, the Gift of Understanding enables us to penetrate deeper into the knowledge of the mystery itself. Our Holy Doctor explains that to know what He is not is to advance in the knowledge of God.[5] The author of the *Imitation* speaks in the same sense as St. Thomas. "We must go beyond all creatures, leaving even ourselves, and there, in the ecstasy of the Spirit, see, O Creator of all things, that no creature can compare with Thee."[6]

---

5.   Ibid., a. 7.

6.   Thomas à Kempis, *The Imitation of Christ, Book* III, chapter 31, 1.

Thus the obscurity of faith remains, but from the bosom of this obscurity there springs a light which, by placing the divine perfection against the imperfection of every created being, gives a kind of negative and analogical intuition of the inaccessible truth.

But what is the good of attempting to define this divine contemplation when we find it stated in the words of St. Catherine herself.

> O Depth, O Deity Eternal, O Profound Ocean, canst Thou give me more than Thyself?...Thou art the Light which surpasses every light. By Thy light Thou gives to the understanding a supernatural light so abundant and so perfect that the light of faith itself is more illumined by it. I see that my soul has light in that faith and that it receives Thy light in that light....Therefore I beg of Thee, Eternal Father, that Thou would illumine me with the light of Holy Faith. That light is an ocean which nourishes the soul as much as it is in Thee....There, where the light of faith abounds, the soul glows, so to speak, with that which it believes. Truly, O Trinity Eternal, Thou hast made me to know and to understand that that sea is a mirror which the hand of Thy love holds before the eyes of my soul and I, Thy creature, see myself in the light of that mirror. Thou presents Thyself to me and I recognize that Thou art the supreme and infinite Good,

the Good beyond all good…the Beauty beyond all beauty, the wisdom beyond all wisdom, for Thou art Wisdom Itself. Who may raise himself toward Thee to thank Thee worthily for the ineffable treasures, both of the superabundant graces which Thou hast granted me and of the doctrine of truth which Thou hast revealed to me beyond the general grace? For this doctrine is a special grace which Thou hast granted to men.

What a difference there is between ordinary faith, always weak and groping, and that faith, certain even intellectually, which, if we may so speak, *sees*!

But how does it see? There cannot be question of such a revelation of the mystery which would transform the gazing of the understanding into an unmixed vision exclusive of faith. Whence then comes that special light which illumines the divine without discovering it?

It is, as we have said, through the heart, that God accomplishes, in this life, the deification of even our intellectual activity. The Holy Spirit, by charity, dwells in our hearts and it is from these that He causes His gifts to shine. The effect of merely human love is to render more intense the act of the intelligence applied to the obtaining of knowledge of the object which we love, to enable it to discover a meaning, hidden but really true, in words, gestures, and every indescribable indication. If love has these instincts, these divinations, the equivalent of lights in the sureness of their insight, when left to its own resources, what must the case of a heart be which is dependent upon God, of which the Holy Spirit has been constituted at all times the director, ruler and guide! Its divine impulses will be infallible, its instinct sure, its intuitions penetrating. The light thus spread abroad by the Holy Spirit is efficacious in its gentleness—*Veni lumen cordium.*

"This act," says Bossuet, "should be performed without effort by a return of the whole heart upon God. It should be, I seek a word to express myself, it should be tender, affectionate, feeling. Do you understand me thoroughly? But do I thoroughly understand myself? For there is a certain movement of the heart which is not at all sensible with a human sensibility but is born of the pure joy of the spirit. And, hence, rejoice and say at all times this alone, 'I consent, my God, to the whole truth of Thy Being. I make it my happiness that Thou art what Thou art: it is my anticipated beatitude. It is my present paradise and will be my paradise in paradise. Amen.'"[7]

Is not this luminous and heartfelt act the very basis of the discourses and acts of St. Catherine? She sees because she loves. It is no longer the simple knowledge of faith: she has loved the Truth which has given her the knowledge of faith: she has tasted it and now she returns to herself with a changed gaze, with that gaze of which the prophet has said: "Taste first and then see"—*Gustate et videte.*[8]

---

7. Bossuet, Discourse to the Sisters of the Visitation.

8. Cf. John of St. Thomas, I-II: q. 70, disp. 18, a. 3, n. 37.

But the Gift of Understanding does not stop there. St. Thomas tells us that it is a gift at once speculative and practical and that its action should be felt in our life. "If it is true, as it is," says Bossuet, "that we are the more active the more we are impelled, animated, and moved by the Holy Spirit, that act by which we give ourselves to Him and the activity which He works in us, place us, so to speak, wholly in action for God."[9] St. Thomas, in a synthesis which is as precise as it is astonishing, has grasped, in the beatitudes of St. Matthew's Gospel, this activity of the Gifts and he has studied to bring to light the correspondence between each of the beatitudes and a Gift of the Holy Spirit. To the Gift of Understanding corresponds "Blessed are the clean of heart for they shall see God." The purification of the heart is the proper work of the Gift of Understanding in this life. The light of vision is the reward of this meritorious purification, a reward which, though it makes itself felt in this world, is wholly achieved only in eternity.

This correspondence between the understanding and purity is a basic trait in the life of St. Catherine. The ecstatic visionary is also the model of penitents. And who more than that ardent saint has cultivated that other purity of the heart which consists in the profession of the Catholic Faith, unmingled with error? Thus, in order that she might see the better, she unceasingly purified her heart by penance and the flight of the

---

9. Discourse on the Act of Abandonment to God (*Discours sur l'Acte de l'Abandon*).

world's prejudices and each degree of contemplation acquired inspired her with the idea of still greater detachment. In her soul there is a twofold action wherein light evokes purity of heart, and purity of heart gives rise to increasing illuminations. In setting forth the bond which unites the Gift of Understanding with the beatitude of the clean of heart St. Thomas has revealed her life to us in a single word.[10]

This is a consoling doctrine for the Gifts of the Holy Spirit are placed in the souls of all the just together with grace and charity. It is for us, under the operation of grace, to use them. But you ask: who will give us this grace? You already have it if you sincerely desire it, for your desire strengthens prayer of which St. Augustine says, "If you are not already attracted, pray to be attracted." Then, to work and say, "I wish to use this Gift of Understanding which I hope is in my soul by the grace of God. St. Catherine help me!"

Then take the Holy Scripture, preferably one of those passages which the Church has chosen in the Liturgy and which it uses to make the interior soul vibrate in the melodies of the plain chant. Or, again, take the psalms, or, in the Gospels, the "Words of the Lord," the "*Verba Domini*" as St. Augustine calls them, such, for example, as "If thou knew the gift of God and who it is that said to thee: Give Me to drink," or, again, "He must increase, but I must decrease." Then, turn toward the interior Guest, the Holy Trinity present in you by

---

10. *Summa Theologiae* II-II, q, 8, a. 7.

grace, or, if you are in Church, toward our Lord present in the tabernacle and consider the words you have chosen as speaking to you of the God you love, as if spoken at that moment for you by the God who lives within you. Taste these words in that presence and, when the movement of your heart returns upon itself in contemplation, you will discover a breadth, height, magnitude, and depth which you had never suspected, which mere faith could not show you, of which only the eye of the heart, a heart in which you hope that the Holy Spirit dwells, will give you understanding.[11]

Then, you will notice how your gaze is obscured by imperfections to which you do not habitually pay heed, by self-love, prejudice, love of ease, false and unchristian ideas, that alloy which even the gold of a pious life contains. As with St. Catherine, the Gift of Understanding will inspire you with a holy hatred of yourself. You will arise stronger with the resolve henceforth to consider "sweet things bitter and bitter things sweet" for the sake of our Lord and to increase, under the guidance of His Spirit, the understanding of the consoling mysteries of our holy faith.

---

11. Though we have the grace, yet knowledge is not certain to one. But we may hope so as long as we are not conscious of a mortal sin and we serve God with a good will. In the case of souls resolutely Christian, the Holy Spirit often adds His testimony to that which results from the witness of conscience. Hence there is a state of practical certitude which, though still leaving room for fear, gives to the activity of the faithful a reassuring basis.

Chapter IX

The Gift of Wisdom

St. Thomas Aquinas

In the "Crucifixion" by Angelico there are two persons which especially draw the attention of the Dominican soul. They are the two saints at the end of the group placed to the right of the cross. In the first row is St. Dominic, kneeling with arms extended in a gesture of grief and compassion. His face, bathed in tears, is but half raised toward the Crucified as if he were still drawn by that sight on the other side of the cross where the Blessed Virgin, supported by John, Magdalene, and Mary, seems about to faint. Standing in the rear row, his arms folded upon his breast with head thrust forward to see the better, is St. Thomas. His face betrays a poignant and concentrated expression. Still he does not weep, he gazes; he gazes fixedly at the Crucified Christ and the mute emotion which envelops him, far from averting his gaze, seems but to deepen it and to draw from the depths of his eyes an intense flame just as, in the black depths of a volcano, one sees the bubbling fiery lava rise, powerful and restrained.

St. Dominic weeps, but with a heart divided between the grief of Christ suffering for souls and the sorrow of souls who, in the Virgin Mary, begin, at the very foot of the Cross, the long martyrdom of their union with the sufferings of Christ; and thus shows the true Apostle, for therein is his double vocation, heartfelt contemplation and merciful communication. Such is the man of the Gift of Knowledge.

St. Thomas looks the fearful sacrifice in the face and, despite the horrors of the torment, masters its characteristics so that nothing may escape him, so that he may more deeply enter into the mystery, and thus he is the Doctor. There is manifested his vocation, no longer divided, but unified in a double faculty, to absorb itself in light, to become itself luminous and, without suspecting it, to give light far and wide. There is the representative of the Gift of Wisdom.

Wisdom, we know, is primarily an intellectual faculty. By it we accustom ourselves to judge everything from on high, from the loftiest possible point, from the divine viewpoint. While Knowledge stops at proximate reasons which can only give a half light, Wisdom, at one bound, has recourse to the supreme explanation. The scientist, in order to explain the harmony of nature, speaks of sidereal revolutions, of orbits, of rotation, etc. He speaks truly but he does not give the ultimate reason. The wise man, whether theologian or philosopher, makes his appeal to the ordaining intelligence of God. With one word he has explained everything although everything is not revealed, for where reason stops, mystery begins.

For this reason the Holy Spirit who "fathoms the depths of God" links us to His own wisdom by a Gift. What a difference there is between the faculty and the Gift! In what does our theology and philosophy consist if not in "finding ignorance in its highest source"? What do we as theologians save to delimit, with more exactitude than others, the boundaries of dark abysses of mysteries or of blinding suns whose centers are inaccessible to the human gaze even when illumined by the obscure light which proceeds from grace? And do not the most intelligent often find their greatest trial in that which even simple souls feel? To find oneself transported by faith before a wall covered with characters which tell of the most sublime and consoling things, and to be unable to pierce the veil which hides them, to realize that we must believe and not be able to see, even for an instant, that which we believe with our whole heart, this is indeed a trial for intelligences as frank as they are faithful. To these it would be more grievous not to believe than not to be able to see.

Where, then, O Doctor of the "Crucifixion," hast thou found that eye which, gazing on the mystery, remains not sightless, glassy and dead, like ours, which, where I lose myself in the void, applies itself to live an unprecedented life, a life which the eye of Archimedes, reflecting the joy of his "Eureka" could not know, nor even Newton, discovering for the first time the mystery of the heavens? Hast thou, O Angelico, in the flight of thy imagination thus transfigured thy model? We cannot imagine it thus. Thou hast seen him. The truth is that the Angelic Painter has comprehended the Angelic Doctor.

O thou, who was so revealed to the soul of Angelico, do thou reveal thyself to us by the power of that holy image, to us who know not how to gaze as thou didst and have so great a need to strengthen our faith by the illumination of the Gifts! Thou didst visibly penetrate the mysteries of the Son of God, incarnate and dying upon the cross. Speak and we will listen to thee. Thine eyes, O Seer, shall be our eyes. Thou hast experienced divine things; do thou disclose to us something of those realities upon which our hearts depend and yet before which our intuitions and our reasonings, as theologians and believers, remain powerless.

The fresco becomes animated and, like to the wave which overflows from the deep basin wherein their gushes forth a living spring, I hear reply that voice, which, of old, satisfied the loving importunities of Brother Reginald, his dearest companion.

"Behold, my son, this Crucified. He is God. He is God incarnate for our sins. For our sins, do you understand? For a long time I have reasoned like a philosopher, it seemed fine for me to behold in the Incarnation of the Word the crown of the Universe, the glory of humanity. I was divided between the Holy Books which everywhere show me the Redemption as the cause of the Incarnation and that sublime idea of a world culminating in a Divine Being, in a Man whose feet should rest upon our earth and his, while his head, loftier than the summits of the highest mountains, should inhabit the inaccessible light of the Deity.[1] But in that moment, all was illumined in the light of the Cross and I saw... the Redemption was the end, the sole end. Why was the Incarnation? For the Redemption. It was not principally to manifest the divine power that a God became incarnate. It was not even to show forth the goodness of God and His divine liberality. It was to manifest His mercy, the most unspeakable of Gis attributes.[2] Now all was explained in the divine word "where sin abounded, pardon superabounded," "He is come to save that which is lost." If man had not sinned He would not have come. Take away sickness, take away wounds, and the doctor is no longer needed. O happy fault to have merited for us such a Redeemer.[3] It was necessary to make the sacrifice of an inferior motive, of a beautiful idea but still only a human idea. Once more I had to bend my understanding beneath the dictates of faith and, behold, through this, I have found anew the light and the highest cause of the mystery is revealed. I had

1.   In *III Sent*. dist. 1.

2.   1, q. 31, a. 3.

3.   *Summa Theologiae* III, q. 1, a. 3.

explained the Incarnation as a man. Now I behold its motive as God sees it. This motive is both our sins and the divine mercy. It is this cross which has revealed it to me and hence I gaze upon it thus.

What a lesson for us too human philosophers and theologians is this intellectual conversion of a St. Thomas, this joyful effacement of the most seductive synthesis before the humble word of the Gospel, of the Apostle, of the Saints! What a lesson it is for us, the faithful, who too often measure the things of God, His teachings, the government of His Church, the conduct of His ministers by the short views that proceed from our pretended lights, our passions, our momentary impressions, or our imagination! Ah! We do not know enough to judge all things, and especially the things of God, the highest cause. We are full of ourselves and, if not at bottom, at least in the real practical affairs of life, in judging, we trouble ourselves with the viewpoint of God little. He has Himself said "Your thoughts are not my thoughts and your ways are not my ways." Yet we must get out of so fatal a habit: the mere zeal for truth requires it.

But, how are we to elevate ourselves sufficiently to consider all things with the eyes of God? Is not such a wisdom reserved for beings totally disengaged from our weaknesses and miseries as are the blessed?

St. Thomas himself reveals to us his secret. It is, he tells us, the Spirit of God alone who really knows the divine mysteries. By our intellectual power we are able to discover some of their features. But what is all our philosophy compared with a single ray which it pleases the Holy Spirit to send us from the bosom of that fullness of light where He dwells? To enter into relationship with the Holy Spirit, there lies the secret of wisdom. But, says the Apostle, "he that adheres to God (listen, by charity) makes but one spirit with His."[4] This does not mean that by love we become the same being as God but that, united to God by a profound sentiment of the heart—not of the heart left to itself, but strengthened, established, by God Himself—we love only that which He loves and enter into a holy and habitual dependence in relation to Him.

The result of this effective dependence ought to make itself especially felt in the conformity of our judgments with His. And, since of ourselves we cannot raise ourselves to the ideas of God, it is necessary that our God, to make His friendship effective, should cause us to partake in the judgments of His wisdom. This it is to form one spirit with God. "It is to be instructed by His unction," as says St. John, "and that in all things"[5] which is to say that the soul, full of the love of God, feels itself gently and, as it were, unctuously touched by higher lights which elevate it to a loftiness of view which it knows not, to a purity, penetration and mastery of its intellectual outlook such that it no longer seems to be of this earth. Just so does the traveler from

---

4.   Ibid., II-II. 45, a. 2.

5.   Ibid.

a mountain peak see everything, the furious sea and the rugged hills, the silent forests and the cities filled with human turmoil, and feels his heart wrapped in the unspeakable joy of being, for a moment, detached from the detail of the earth and able to dominate it with a single glance.

Nothing is so restful as such a sight which abounds in salutary reflections. The smallness of that which ordinarily arouses our passions appears to us in all its reality. The soul which sees from above is at one stroke enlarged and quieted. That doubtless is the reason why St. Augustine has linked to the Gift of Wisdom the beatitude of the peacemakers, "Blessed are the peacemakers for they shall be called the children of God."[6] Peace is nothing other than the tranquility of order. But that alone is capable of assuring order which sees the detail in the whole, which judges from a loftier viewpoint that which is great and that which is small. To make one's life peaceful, to make the lives of others the same, it is absolutely essential to be lifted above oneself, above everything and to judge oneself in the truth. But how is this to be done? We cannot separate ourselves from ourselves and we needs must live in the world. How then are we to raise ourselves above ourselves? Where is the mountain whence, with detached and dominating glance, we may truly appreciate our life and that of others?

This mountain is God. God dominates His creation by nature. Those alone to whom He communi-

---

6.   Ibid., a. 6.

cates His judgment can dominate and judge all as God does. And that is why, in the Gospel, the figure of the Son of God made man appears to us with a unique expression both of dominance and of peace. He is a wise man; He judges others with thoughts other than our own, with thoughts quite simply spoken but filled with a content which compels the wise men of all time to reflect. But in dominating us, He does not crush us; He does not break the bruised reed; He does not quench the still smoking flax. This wise man is a peacemaker. The Divinity which dwells within Him is like a peak from which He considers and judges, in their reality, all the causes of our troubles and strife; whence He causes order, tranquility, and peace to radiate into the souls of those who believe His word. There lies the model.

He is also the reward for He has said "Blessed are the peacemakers for they shall be called the children of God." Yes, something of that serene and intelligent domination, of that tranquil order, which characterized the face of the Son of God, passed into the wise men of the earth and humanity, struck with the resemblance, proclaimed it with a loud voice.

Behold St. Thomas Aquinas! What theologian, in the judgments upon all things divine and human in whose formulation he spent his entire life, more attached himself to the very thought of God? Who is wiser with the wisdom which comes from on high? Yet where is there a more intelligently serene countenance, a more peaceful life, and a more tranquilizing work?

No, after the Gospel, after the Apostle, there is no reading which manifests to the spirit the impression of tranquility in order as does that of the works of St. Thomas. Jesus saw; St. Thomas reasoned. There lies the difference and it is immense. But their spirits seem to be—dare I say it—related. Simplicity and profundity, universality and the least detail, sublimity and condescension, the hall mark of the Gospel, are all to be found, in a lesser but still in an eminent degree, in the works of St. Thomas. Is not this a proof of the law laid down by the Holy Spirit Himself: "He who adheres to God makes but one spirit with Him." And is not the resemblance between the intelligent and serene countenance of the Angelic Doctor and the intellectual mien of our Lord the realization of the promise of good fortune made to the wise? "Blessed are the peacemakers for they shall be called the children of God."

Chapter X

The Gifts of the Holy Spirit in the Most Pure Heart of the Virgin Mary

SALVE REGINA! This is the cry which most joyfully rises from the hearts of all the children of the Blessed Dominic. Each evening the saints of our Order have had it upon their lips. Mary is their Queen. What does this imply? Evidently only a spiritual royalty. But what gifts can assure such a royalty but the Gifts of the Spirit? It is through her heart, inflamed with an eminent charity, the dwelling chosen above all by the Holy Spirit, that Mary reigns over hearts themselves filled with charity and the indwelling of the Holy Spirit. In her we can no longer single out, as in each of our Saints, some one particular Gift. The Spouse of the Holy Spirit has entered into the plenitude of all the Gifts. The Seven Gifts of the Holy Spirit shine forth from her Most Pure Heart and make it a resplendent and incomparable glory. Ye Blessed of the Order of St. Dominic, each one adorned with a precious but special Gift, salute your Queen! *Salve Regina!*

Being eager to know the mysteries of the Most Pure Heart of the Blessed Virgin, St. Bernard anxiously sought to know how he could penetrate its depths. It seemed to him that he found a certain indication in the phrase from the Gospel "A good man draws good things from the treasure of his heart." He then recalled that the Gospel itself has recorded for us exactly seven phrases of the Blessed Virgin. She spoke twice to the angel, twice to Elizabeth, twice to her Divine Son, and once to the servants at the feast in Cana. Here then, he cries, are the seven acts of love which reveal her treasure, the seven flames of her Heart. The first is that of the love which separates, the second is that of transforming love, the third that of the love which gives itself, the fourth, that of love in rejoicing, the fifth that of restful love, the sixth that of compassionating love, while the seventh is that of consummative love.[1]

These characteristics of the degrees of love of the Most Pure Heart of the Most Holy Virgin appear to us to correspond to the different Gifts of the Holy Spirit, although the order accepted by St. Bernard may perhaps be capable of rearrangement, especially in regard to the fourth "flame," the "*amor jubilans*," which corresponds to the canticle "*Magnificat*," and which we transfer to the seventh place, as giving the last word of that heart. Be that as it may, one cannot find a more authentic basis on which to speak of the mysterious operations of the

---

1. Sermon IV, "On the Visitation." Office of the Most Pure Heart of the Blessed Virgin Mary, Lessons of the Second Nocturn.

Holy Spirit in the heart of Mary than these words recorded in the Gospel. We will apply ourselves, then, to meditate upon them in order to discover their secrets.

First Word: The Gift of Fear

> The angel said to her: "Fear not, Mary, for thou hast found grace with God. Behold thou shalt conceive in thy womb and shall bring forth a Son and thou shalt call His Name Jesus." Mary said to the Angel: "How shall this be done because I know not Man?"[2]

"Fear not Mary." These words of the angel place us, right at the beginning, upon our way. Mary was troubled at the sight of him and she asked the meaning of his salutation. "Fear not Mary for thou hast found grace with God," and the angel outlined the glories of the divine grace. She should bear a son. Jesus should be great and be called the Son of the Most High and the Lord God would give Him the throne of His father David. He should reign over the house of Jacob forever and of His kingdom there should be no end. This message could only redouble the fear of Mary, but her answer explains to us the nature of her fear. It is the fear of a child of God, of a chaste virgin, who, under the inspiration of the Spirit, had vowed her virginity to the Most High; to

---

2. Luke 1:30–34.

please Him she had forever separated herself from every worldly hope. Her cry is the cry of the love which separates, that is to say, of the Gift of Filial Fear which casts far from the just all which may distract him from God. "How shall this be done because I know not man?"

"Blessed are the poor in spirit for theirs is the kingdom of heaven." Mary is poor in spirit; she has stripped herself of every created good, including that hope which made the heart of every daughter of Israel beat and made them regard virginity as a disgrace. She had renounced marriage and, even after the message of the angel, she intended to remain a virgin. Thus the beatitude, reserved to those who through fear of God are poor in spirit, was to be fulfilled in her. The kingdom of heaven is hers since Jesus, the great King of that realm, descends to become incarnate in her womb.

Second Word: The Gift of Fortitude

> The angel answering said to her: "The Holy Spirit shall come upon thee and the power of the Most High shall overshadow thee. Therefore the Holy which shall be born of thee shall be called the Son of God." Mary said: "Behold the handmaid of the Lord: be it done to me according to thy word."[3]

3. Luke 1:35–38.

What a transformation! Unquiet hesitation is sup-
planted by absolute confidence, the resolve to abandon
oneself without reserve to the action of God who can do
all things, who clears away all dangers and who brings
us surely to the most inaccessible end. How could she
preserve her virginity and yet become a mother? The angel answers: "Nothing is impossible to God." And Mary
said: "Behold the handmaid of the Lord: be it done to
me according to thy word." This is a cry of transforming
love, that is to say of the Gift of Fortitude. "The Holy
Spirit," says St. Thomas, "often moves the spirit of man
in such a way that he performs his work while avoid-
ing all the perils which menace him. Although it is not
within the power of man to attain the end or escape
the peril...the Holy Spirit, who has the guidance of our
march toward eternal life, intervenes and produces in
the soul an assurance which excludes all contrary fear.
This gift of the Holy Spirit is the Gift of Fortitude."[4] Is
not this passage from the Holy Doctor the literal commentary upon the transformation produced in Mary.
She, troubled, said, "How shall this be done?" The angel
answered her: "The power of the Most High shall over-
shadow thee.... Nothing is impossible with God." The
spirit of Fortitude inspired her and, like a disciplined
soldier, she answered: "Behold the handmaid of the
Lord: be it done to me according to thy word."

"Blessed are they who hunger and thirst after
justice, for they shall be filled." This is the beatitude

---

4.   *Summa Theologiae* II-II, q. 139, a. 1.

THE GIFTS OF THE HOLY SPIRIT IN THE DOMINICAN SAINTS

which St. Augustine connects with the Gift of Fortitude. Mary truly hungered and thirsted after justice,
since, when faced with the realization in her of the
great promise to Israel, she maintained the rights of
the promise of virginity made to God. Behold Blessed Mary filled! She begot the Messiah and remained
a Virgin. The Holy Child who was born of her was
called the Son of God. O happy and blessed Mary, ever
Virgin and Mother of God.

Third Word: The Gift of Piety

> And Mary rising up in those days, went into
> the hill country with haste into a city of Juda
> and she entered into the house of Zachary and
> saluted Elizabeth. And it came to pass that
> when Elizabeth heard the salutation of Mary,
> the infant leaped in her womb. And Elizabeth
> was filled with the Holy Spirit; and she cried
> out with a loud voice and said: "Blessed art
> thou among women and blessed is the fruit of
> thy womb."[5]

She saluted Elizabeth. What this salutation was,
the Gospel does not say. It was the cry of the love which
communicates itself, which, possessing some good,
seeks only to share it. And, behold, it is immediately

5. Luke 1:39–42.

114

shared. The child of Elizabeth, a symbol of all humanity, leaps in the womb of its mother and its mother is
filled with the spirit which dwells in Mary. The spirit of
Mary saluting Elizabeth is the spirit of piety, for piety
is that gift of God which causes us to revere not only
God, the Father of the Christian Family, but that family itself in all its members, to render to it all the duties
we owe, to communicate to it the best we have. This is
exactly what Mary did, going in haste across the mountains to lend her aid to her cousin Elizabeth, to rejoice
the heart of the mother by the presage of the Blessed
One of Israel, to sanctify, in advance, the Precursor, the
Herald of the future sanctification of humanity. So also
the latter, by the mouth of Elizabeth, acknowledged
the piety which had inspired Mary's journey: "Blessed
art thou among women and blessed is the fruit of thy
womb." "And whence is this to me that the mother of
my Lord should come to me?" "Blessed art thou who
has believed because those things shall be accomplished
that were spoken to thee by the Lord."

Yes, happy and blessed is Mary! According to St.
Thomas the beatitudes of the Gospel vie with one another for the honor of setting in relief the Gift of Piety,
doubtless because this excellent Gift cannot be exer-
cised without raising in its passage a train of excellent
desires. Blessed are the meek for they shall possess the
land: blessed are they that hunger and thirst after justice
for they shall be filled: blessed are the merciful for they
shall obtain mercy. The act of the Gift of the Piety is

formed of what is best in the three gifts of meekness, justice, and mercy. Indeed all these are present in the Visitation of Mary. Her salutation was meek; witness the welcome which Elizabeth gave her; her visit was an act of justice since she was fulfilling a duty; the work of sanctification which she performed was full of mercy. Behold her, then, who at one stroke possesses the land by the sanctification which she there produced, who is filled by the joy which her visit produces, who sees the mercy of the Lord confirmed in her by the new assurance added to her happiness by the prophecy of Elizabeth: "Blessed art thou that hast believed, because those things shall be accomplished which were spoken to thee by God."

Fourth Word: The Gift of Counsel

> And the third day there was a marriage in Cana of Galilee, and the mother of Jesus was there. And Jesus also was invited and His disciples to the marriage. And the wine failing, the Mother of Jesus said to Him: "They have no wine." And Jesus said to her: "Woman, what is that to Me and to thee. My hour is not yet come."[6]

"They have no wine." How much confidence there is in this laconic saying of the Mother to the Son!

6. John 2:1–4.

She urges nothing; she does not even make a request; knowing His Heart, she contents herself with opening hers. Yes, it is her heart that she opens, the heart of the housewife and guest delicately moved by the sorrows which her host is about to experience. "They have no wine": it is the hardly murmured counsel of a mother conscious of the heart and the omnipotence of her Son, which completely rest the one upon the other, "*flamma amoris soporantis.*" Who could have inspired in her a delicacy at once so insinuating and so firm, so worthy of God to whom she spoke, for it is God whom she is venturing to counsel, yet so truly marked with the stamp of a mother's rights? If ever counsel was derived from a gift to mortal, it was truly in this circumstance. What man, of himself, could discover the persuasive power of such a counsel? Is it not the act of a prudence counseled from above, of a prudence directed by the great Counselor?

"Blessed are the merciful for they shall obtain mercy." It would seem, at first sight, that Mary has not obtained mercy. "Woman," Jesus said to her, "what is that to Me and to thee. My hour is not yet come." But this is only apparently so. Mothers know what is hidden beneath the exterior coldness which their grown sons raise to their overtures. They know that while they, in the name of reason, resist, yet in their hearts they have already yielded. Mary was not mistaken. Her heart, full of pity for these poor people, knew that it had obtained pity. She ordered the servants to do all that her Son should bid and the miracle was performed. Her counsel had prevailed, because fundamentally, it was the counsel of a love inspired by the God of Mercy.

Fifth Word: The Gift of Knowledge

> And Jesus said to her: "Woman, what is that to Me and to thee, My hour is not yet come." His mother said to the waiters: "Whatsoever He shall say to you do ye." Jesus said to them: "Fill the water pots with water, and they filled them up to the brim." And Jesus said to them: "Draw out now and carry to the chief steward of the feast." And they carried it. And when the chief steward had tasted the water made wine...he call the bridegroom and said to him: "Every man at first sets forth good wine and, when men have well drunk, then that which is worse. But thou hast kept the good wine until now."[7]

"My hour is not yet come," said Jesus. But that of Mary had come and she knew it. The hour of Mary is that in which man finds himself in embarrassment, chagrin, or misery. She knows all our sufferings from the little wound to the self-esteem of the host who, in the midst of the banquet, discovers that he has noth-

7. John 2:4–10.

ing more to offer his guests, to those dolorous sufferings which attack our life at its roots. She knows all this and her knowledge is not inactive, "*flamma amoris compatientis.*" It is the frame of compassionating love. "Whatsoever He shall say to you do ye," she said to the servants. Who could have inspired this boldness in her? When the Master had said "My hour is not yet come," how dare she act as if it had come? It is the Spirit from on High who animates her with a higher knowledge. It is because beneath the harsh phrase "Woman, what is that to thee and to Me?" she, by the inspiration of the Spirit, discovers the heart of Him who should soon say "I have compassion upon the multitude." (*Misereor super turbam.*)

"Blessed are they that weep, for they shall be comforted." This is the beatitude which St. Augustine links with the Gift of Knowledge and justly so for the better one knows the world the more one sees that it is sorrowful and full of misery.

The delicate heart of Mary discovered in the sorrow of the bridegroom a human grief. It is small but it is enough when one is inspired by the Gift of Knowledge. She knows and she weeps with those who weep. "They have no wine." What a pitiful plea! But, immediately, "Whatsoever He shall say to you do ye." The water is turned into wine and the anxiety which had weighed down the heart of the unhappy host is turned into a great gladness. And Mary rejoiced greatly at hearing the chief steward of the feast, who suspected nothing, say to the bridegroom: "Thou hast kept the good wine till now." What a consolation to her delicate heart. Blessed are they that weep, instructed by the Gift of Knowledge, for they shall be comforted.

Sixth Word: The Gift of Understanding

> And it came to pass that after three days they found Him in the Temple sitting in the midst of the doctors, hearing them and asking them questions. And all that heard Him were astonished at His wisdom and His answers. And seeing Him they wondered, and His mother said to Him: "Son, why hast Thou done so to us? Behold Thy father and I have sought Thee sorrowing." And He said to them: "How is it that you sought Me? Did you not know that I must be about My Father's business?" And they understood not the word which He spoke unto them. And He went down with them and came to Nazareth and was subject to them. And His mother kept all these words in her heart."[8]

"Son, why hast Thou done so to us?" Is there Understanding here? "And they understood not the word which He spoke to them." Can this be called Under-

---

8. Luke 2:46–51.

standing? We have not read the text to the end: "His mother kept all these words in her heart." Here is the work of the Gift of Understanding.

To find we must seek; to receive we must ask. In the Canticle of Canticles wherein the saints have recognized the embraces of the human understanding and the Divinity, there are words denoting search and moments of meeting, fugitive meetings and silent possessings. Mary is the Spouse of the Canticle: Jesus is her Well-Beloved. She knows Him by the spirit of Understanding which was bestowed upon her at the Annunciation. Yet, the Gift of Understanding, upon this earth, does not exclude the obscurities of faith. The soul sees suddenly, under a mighty impulse of the heart, but a moment later the Beloved is hidden. It can no longer lay hold upon Him and it goes in search of Him.

> "I sought Him whom my soul loves.
> I sought Him and found Him not.
> I will arise and go about the city,
> In the streets and in the broad ways
> I will seek Him whom my soul loves.
> The watchmen who keep the city found me,
> Have you seen Him whom my soul loves?
> When I had a little passed by them
> I found Him whom my soul loves."[9]

---

9. Song of Songs 3:1–4.

It is with this figurative paraphrase in mind that we should read our text. Even in Mary, the Gift of Understanding does not exclude momentary lack of understanding. It even requires it, so as to provoke an anxious search, to arouse, because of the absence of God, the Beloved, a stronger movement of the heart which translates itself into a more ardent flame: "*flamma amoris consummantis.*" "Have you seen Him whom my soul loves?" said the Spouse to the keepers of the city. Mary said to her Son: "Behold, Thy father and I have sought Thee sorrowing."

Jesus replies by recalling His Divine Paternity: and, says the Gospel, "they understood not the word which He spoke to them." Joseph and Mary did not immediately understand, but, like the Spouse of the Canticles who, when she had passed the watchmen, found Him whom her soul loved, Mary is shown to us keeping all these things in her heart. Does this mean that she, at last, understands? No, that is not possible. But she does better: she sees. She sees with those eyes of the soul which do not exclude obscurity but rather give an understanding more immediate and more certain than the clearness of evidence.

She does not understand, but, under the inspiration of the Spirit, she feels the joy of being the Spouse of the Eternal Father who is the Father of her Son, and of being the mother of that Son who is already about His Father's business: she feels it intimately, silently: she keeps it in her heart.

"Blessed are the pure in heart, for they shall see God." The heart of Mary was most pure. She has no other love than the Father, Son, and Spirit. She lives by the understanding of the deepest mysteries of the Divinity. That is why she is blessed.

Seventh Word: The Gift of Wisdom

"My soul doth magnify the Lord."
Magnificat anima mea Dominum.[10]

This is the Canticle of Mary, the flame of love in rejoicing, as St. Bernard says. It is the utterance of the enthusiasm which is born in the lowest depths of a heart wherein God has established His dominion in an absolute and royal way. Such a heart sees God everywhere, in all the events of its life, in all the sources of the history of the world. God becomes, for it, the great fundamental reality who hides Himself under the vesture of things. In Him and by Him, we live and move and have our being. The soul judges everything by this Supreme Cause, infinite and profound. It seeks to enter into communication with the Wisdom which rules the world, to identify its own views with His. And since this inspiration arises from its charity, whose government the Holy Spirit regulates, nothing can hinder this identification becoming a reality.

10. Luke 1:46–55.

For this reason the Gift of Wisdom exists, the Gift of those peaceful enthusiasts who feel that the God who governs the world is with them and they wish to spread this conviction throughout the entire world. It is He who rested upon Mary at the moment when, filled with the Spirit of God, after this same Spirit had enveloped Elizabeth and the child, the symbol of humanity, had leaped in the womb, she burst forth into that Canticle wherein the love of God appears at each turn of the discourse. It is the ultimate expression of her Most Pure Heart.

> My soul doth magnify the Lord and my spirit hath rejoiced in God my Savior, because He hath regarded the humility of His handmaid.
>
> For, behold, from henceforth, all generations shall call me blessed, because He that is mighty hath done great things to me.
>
> Holy is His Name, and His Mercy is from generation to generation to them that fear Him.
>
> He hath showed might in His arm: He hath scattered the proud in the conceit of their heart.
>
> He hath put down the mighty from their seat and hath exalted the humble.

He hath filled the hungry with good things and the rich He hath sent empty away.

He hath received Israel His servant, being mindful of His Mercy as He spoke to our fathers, to Abraham and His seed forever."

Chapter XI

The Gifts in Heaven

The Dominican Pentecost

The Holy City, the celestial Jerusalem, is not watered by the course of a stream like to those on earth; but, springing from the source of life, the Holy Spirit, of which a feeble drop waters us here below, floods the blessed spirits with the effervescent flow of the seven spiritual forces.[1]

It is in these terms that St. Ambrose affirms the permanence, and describes the abundance, of the Gifts of the Holy Spirit in heaven.

In heaven, the moral virtues have no longer any reason for existence; there hope is accomplished, faith is placed in the light of glory; all these virtues disappear with our earthly life: charity alone remains. It remains

---

1. St. Ambrose, *On the Holy Spirit*, I.16, cited by St. Thomas in *Summa Theologiae* I-II, q. 68, a. 6.

the same, but infinitely more burning, since it is no longer nourished in the obscurity of faith but in the vision, face to face, of the Eternal Beauty.

Charity remains: that is to say, that the Holy Spirit does not cease to dwell in the soul of the blessed: only it is no longer as a bias far from its center of attraction and which encounters all kinds of obstacles, but as a bias arrived at its destination which exerts an influence henceforth untrammeled and indissolubly establishing the being which it animates to the end of its efforts.

If, then, the Holy Spirit reigns more than ever in the heart of the blessed one it is because the Gifts do not cease to regulate its new activity. What, indeed, is the reason for these Gifts? We have told this before: it is to make the soul docile to the moving of the Holy Spirit. But when will it be more responsive to this moving than when it has arrived in that country where God is all in all, "*omnia in omnibus*," and man is totally subjected to God?[2]

But if the Gifts exist in heaven, their field of action is greatly modified. In heaven there are no longer the delays which hope knows, the obscurity which faith implies, which makes us understand and not see the mysteries of God, no longer the impetuosities which impede the sureness of our counsel, no longer ignorances to be overcome by mortification, works of mercy to perform, adversity to be borne, pride to be restrained by salutary fears. The Gifts aid us to overcome all these

2. Ibid.

difficulties of life. But the difficulties no longer exist. Hence says St. Gregory the Great, we admit that there is in each of the Gifts something which disappears with the present life.[3]

But he immediately adds that something remains and that it is not the least glorious function of the Gifts.

The Gift of Wisdom continues to fill the heart of the blessed with Divine Certitudes: the Gift of Understanding illumines it more than ever: Counsel fills the soul with rational satisfactions: the Gift of Fortitude fills it with assurance: the Gift of Knowledge enlightens it to its depths: Piety inspires it with sentiments of expansive gratitude: the Gift of Fear enjoys without constraint the joys of fulfillment.

***

The Blessed Virgin Mary was the first to receive the imprint of these gifts thus transformed. The holy apprehensions and courageous decision of the Annunciation, the merciful salutation of the Visitation, the compassionate counsel and knowledge of her Son's ways at the wedding of Cana, the silent recollection in the understanding of the mystery of the Divine Paternity, the exaltation of the "*Magnificat:,*" all this is reflected in the heart and is recognizable in the expression of her countenance, but how much more strikingly. She is still the Virgin of the Seven Words of the

---

3. Ibid., ad 2.

Gospel, but that which was formerly veiled, like all human merit, is now resplendent. The ideal of her heart is discovered. O my good Mother, how fair thou art! "*Tota pulchra est.*"

Mary has opened her mantle, that mantle which envelops the universe with her protective power, and in that best of places, wherein St. Dominic discovered them like little birds beneath the wings of their mother, are our Saints.

***

St. Dominic! He is no longer the Dominic of the "Crucifixion"; no longer the scholar who, kneeling at the foot of the cross, weeps over the sins and miseries whose depths have been made known to him by the Gift of Knowledge. He is the Dominic of the "*Incoronazione*," the star erect and flaming upon his brow, the glance fixed upon the Thrice Holy God, plunging into the divine origins of the salvation of the world. His look has become serene after the complete evidence of the goodness which watches over the salvation of sinners. Beside him is his son of predilection, St. Hyacinth, the Apostle of a race of martyrs, the Saint who gazes ever toward the east of Europe and ceases not to pray for that nation which has been his lot. He partakes in the serene joy of his Father, for he sees plainly the eternal decree which ordains that the blood of the martyrs be the seed of Christians. Upon his brow is a tiny star, the image of that of his blessed Father, the image also of his destiny which is to gravitate toward the great Dominican star. This is the first constellation beneath the mantle of the Queen of our Order.

***

St. Catherine of Siena, St. Agnes of Montepulciano, St. Rose of Lima, and St. Catherine de Ricci form a chosen group wherein the brilliancies of understanding, the glitterings of filial fear, the gentle light of piety and the reanimating ardors of fortitude blend their diverse harmonies into a mighty concord, indefinable and beatifying. Thus it is that on a fine summer night, the traveler along those seas in which the stars are reflected from the promontory can contemplate in prayer the vivid twinkling of the heavens. Suddenly toward the south, a trapezoidal group of four shining stars emerges from the line of the horizon and slowly mounts, filling that corner of the heaven with a white brilliancy. In front is a star of the first magnitude, one of the most brilliant in the heavens. It is Spica of Virgo and its three followers. Such is Catherine of Siena and her three sisters. There, standing out upon the somber blue background of the mantle of the Queen of the Friars Preachers is the second constellation.

***

In the heavens there are stars, like Sirius, with empurpled and bloody fires. It is with this brilliance that our martyrs, St. Peter of Verona and St. John of Gorcum shine. Their countenance reflects fortitude, but no longer the fortitude of victory yet to be achieved. They smile, as at a game, upon the strife of their martyrdom now that they see clearly that they were right not to be afraid, now that they behold, in its source, the strength which sustained them, the omnipotence of the Eternal. There, beneath the mantle of Mary, is the empurpling of a third constellation.

***

Now come the Apostle Preachers. Their soul is no longer oppressed by the salutary terrors that the Spirit inspired in them "lest having preached to others, they themselves should be cast away."[4] They have ceased to "realize in their body the filling up of what was wanting in the Passion of Christ." There shine the glories of the two Spanish Apostles who divided the world between them, St. Vincent Ferrer and St. Louis Bertrand. St. Vincent is no longer terrifying and St. Louis Bertrand no longer trembles, for before them stretches eternally the ocean of the Divine Mercy. This is the fourth constellation in the heaven of the Mantle of Mary.

***

4.   1 Cor. 9:27.

Glory to the Holy Trinity! Behold the constellation of the Doctors. Here is their old friend, the Holy and Indivisible Essence of God. How they have searched into It as long as they lived. How great was their labor! "For Thy sake, they sang, we are mortified [slain] all the day: we are as sheep for the slaughter." The altar of sacrifice was their work table: their mortification was their intellectual labor, elevated to the service of the Faith. St. Raymond, St. Antoninus, what a gaze is yours! How sparkling it is, how intense: how it devours, how eagerly it feasts!

But what is that inexpressible light, shining behind you like a blazing golden fire? The whole mantle of the Virgin is illumined by it, all the celestial beings see its warm light mingle with theirs. As in the "Crucifixion" of Angelico, it is in the last row. St. Thomas Aquinas in ecstasy: his gaze, open as a bottomless gulf, gives entrance of full extent to the waves of light which flow to Him from the Holy Trinity! The glory of God is engulfed in his vast intellect and descends to his very heart and did not his breast glow like a sun and cause all this flame one might believe him swallowed up in it. "An immortal sun springs from his breast." And upon the mantle of the Blessed Virgin the fifth Dominican constellation shines as the sun.

***

The heaven of our Mother's mantle, beyond these stars of the first magnitude, is not a void. A hidden light fills it and the eye, which gazes at it fixedly, feels that every moment it sees the twinkling of an infinite number of lesser stars. It is not deceived, for the very depths of the Virgin's mantle are alive: one sees an infinite number of Dominican souls. Some of them are even recognizable: they are the protectors of our Order, our Beati. There, too, are all our brothers and sisters who, from the time of St. Dominic, have died in the Lord to the singing of the "*Salve Regina*"; there also are our faithful brothers and sisters of the Third Order whose hearts beat in union with ours. Shining there are our benefactors, associated in our suffrages, officially or not it matters little so long as they have been with us in our works and our merits. With them are the innumerable host of souls devoted to the Rosary, the Confraternity of the Blessed Sacrament, the Holy Name and the Angelic warfare. Together with these we find the doctors who have professed our doctrine and, like the children of St. Teresa and their mother herself, "have deserved so well of it." As a further glory we find the multitude of souls saved by our preaching, our prayers, our mortifications, and our good works. And there is throughout the whole Dominican heaven a profound light, a joyful twinkling, an intense and diffusive animation which makes the brilliance of the stars of the first line stand out, just as on a bright night, the splendid pathway of the Milky Way shines through the whole heavens as a living and lucid base from which the great constellations are detached and evolved.

***

You holy, pious Dominican souls, the mantle of your Mother awaits you. Why delay longer in following with docility the inspirations of that Spirit who has espoused Mary and by which all your Saints have lived? You are hesitating, depressed, weak, and afraid of the supernatural. Should you be afraid of the Holy Spirit which made Mary so excellent and our brethren so amiable and so holy? "For you have not received the spirit of bondage again in fear, but you have received the spirit of adoption of sons, whereby we cry Abba (Father). For the Spirit Himself giveth testimony to our spirit that we are the sons of God. And if sons, heirs also; heirs indeed of God, and joint-heirs with Christ: yet so, if we suffer with Him, that we may be also glorified with Him."[5] You do not know how to act nor where to begin? Leave that to the Spirit. He has charged Himself with our conduct. Listen again to St. Paul: "Likewise the Spirit also helps our infirmity. For we know not what we should pray for as we ought; but the Spirit Himself asks for us with unspeakable groanings. And He that searches the hearts, knows what the Spirit desires: because He asks for the saints according to God."[6]

Recollect, then, upon this holy day of Pentecost, the anniversary of the glorious day upon which the Holy Spirit took possession of the world: recall, then,

---

5. Romans 8:15–17.

6. Romans 8:26–27.

in the presence of the Holy Virgin Mary, Spouse of the Holy Spirit, all the Saints of our Order, who were His confidants, His friends, His faithful disciples and ask the Holy Spirit, who dwells in you, to intercede on your behalf with one of those unspeakable groanings which obtain from God sanctity.

> *Veni Sancte Spiritus*
> *Et emitte coelitus*
> *Lucis tuae radium.*[7]

---

7.   Come, Holy Spirit, and from Thy clear celestial height, Thy beaming radiance give.

Made in the USA
Middletown, DE
15 April 2019